give me that
Prime-Time
Religion

give me that

Prime-Time
Religion

an insider's report on the
ORAL ROBERTS
Evangelistic Association

by Jerry Sholes

HAWTHORN BOOKS

A division of Elsevier-Dutton Publishing Company
New York

GIVE ME THAT PRIME-TIME RELIGION

Library of Congress Catalog Card Number: 79-3168

ISBN: 0-8015-3091-1

1 2 3 4 5 6 7 8 9 10

This book is dedicated to my parents,
the Rev. and Mrs. Bruce A. Sholes.

FOREWORD

This book may upset some people. It might even make them angry. If it causes them to take a closer look at BIG RELIGION for what it really is, then so much the better. If it causes people to stop watching paid religious programming on Sunday morning...and go, instead, to the church of their choice in their own community, then I'll really feel like this book achieved its purpose.

Some will conclude that the purpose of this book is to attack religion in general and Oral Roberts in particular. That isn't true. I was brought up in the church...my own father was a minister...and I have very strong beliefs about the validity of the church *at the community level*. Nothing will ever change those beliefs.

With the advent of electronic religion, however, the church has been artificially extended into our homes. The offering plate that gets passed by televised religion has grown so large that it includes the contributions of millions of dollars by millions of people. When you endeavor to trace the "good" that those contributions do, you begin to run into muddy water. A local church does *good* in its community. A large television ministry tends to localize its funds in and around whatever project the television minister wants to "push." No real good ever finds its way back into the communities of those millions who contribute to large television ministries.

What *does happen* is that television ministers enjoy extremely high standards of living...million dollar homes, expensive cars, big business deals, computerized mailing lists, and cash flow patterns that boggle the mind! You begin to suspect that the entire pattern of large electronic ministries is much more closely related to the ego of the television minister than to anything else.

If I accomplish anything with this book, it will simply be to put some of you addicted television Christians back into your local churches on Sunday morning. And every clear thinking pastor in the country will say, "Praise God!"

PROLOGUE

What kind of person writes a book about Oral Roberts? Well, *this* person wrote a book about Oral Roberts because he came to know him rather well after having worked with him for three and a half years. I joined Oral Roberts as a television writer in January 1975...when the decision was made to produce his television programs in Tulsa rather than at NBC studios. I wrote television shows for Oral Roberts and eventually became his Associate Producer. I managed one of the largest television studios in the country for him and all we ever did was produce programs for Oral Roberts.

As a writer, I was also an idea man who was often called upon to provide a good idea for various elements of Oral's ministry. No one will ever find my name on the credit crawl of Oral's television shows as a writer. The term "writer" conveys an impression that perhaps something might be contrived... rather than inspired by God. That's why I was never called a writer! Still, I did write for Oral Roberts: I wrote the openings for his television shows, I wrote book offers for him, I wrote the quarterly prime time specials (which even included selecting music), and I put words in Oral's mouth. Maybe God inspired me. While I'm not about to discuss that point, it is important for readers of this book to understand that I did have to work closely with Oral Roberts and that I, personally, came to understand him as a human being.

And that's really what this book is all about. Oral Roberts is a little too much of a human being! He has many faces and the one you see on television is just one of them. That particular face isn't too bad. Some of his other faces are and that's what some of the chapters of this book deal with...the other faces of Oral Roberts.

I feel, as the author of this book, that it's very important that Christian readers learn of *my* background and understand why I would write a book which criticizes someone like an Oral Roberts. First off, I grew up in the church and sat on the front pew of my father's church on many a Sunday.

morning. My father was a minister whom I always admired... and still do. He spent his entire life helping other people and even now, as a retiree, keeps himself busy in various church activities. I reveal this merely to indicate that I don't harbor deep negative feelings about the church or ministers.

My own professional background has always been in public relations, fund raising, or administration in large universities. I was on the staff of Iowa State University from 1966 through 1970, and also worked at the University of Florida from 1970 through 1973. I *know* what a university is and I have very strong feelings about the role of higher education in this country. I've been through some tough times at both the above institutions...through sit-ins, demonstrations, black athlete boycotts, and the trial of the Gainesville Eight. But I never saw anything at either of those two institutions which distressed me as much as what goes on at Oral Roberts University...in the name of Christianity.

Any university can experience two rather broad types of problems with its student body: one is externally created and the other is brought about internally by the institutional environment. Most universities in the sixties went through problems created externally...by the attitudes which incoming students brought with them as they matriculated. The war in Viet Nam, for example, had nothing to do with higher education...but colleges and universities became arenas for protest. Alumni and parents blamed the universities. University administrators blamed the parents. And the parents *were* at fault...as was the society they helped to create.

One of the finest men I've ever known, President Robert Parks of Iowa State University, made the following paraphrased comment: "If parents allow their children to grow up without any guidance, any reprimands, and allow them to express themselves in any way they choose, then I fail to understand why those same parents should expect a university president to take a ball bat to their kids when they get out of hand."

XII

He was saying that the universities were inheriting problems that society and parents had helped create. Universities, caught up in changing times, and still trying to operate under the doctrine of *in loco parentis*, found themselves adversely enmeshed in unwanted and undeserved publicity. In spite of all that turmoil and all the backlash that many universities felt, those institutions survived and prospered. Many of the students who were so vocal in protesting *everything* in the sixties have grown up and used what they learned and have become the budding leaders of the next decade. The reason is very simple: the product which those embroiled institutions offered was a good one and their students benefited by it in spite of all the problems they either created or encountered. Those institutions had good curricula, taught by competent faculty who knew what they knew and knew how to teach it. I have never been more proud of anything than I am of being an alumnus of Iowa State University. I can look back on the days when a young man named Don Smith was student body president at Iowa State. He claimed that he would bring Iowa State, kicking and screaming, into the twentieth century. Well, Don Smith grew up. *He* kicked and *he* screamed and Iowa State brought *him* into the twentieth century. *He grew up*.

On the other hand, Oral Roberts University, with its garish architecture and its strict Code of Honor and dress codes, does not allow its students to grow up. They aren't allowed to question. They are *told*. Abnormal behavior such as not wearing a tie to classes will ultimately lead to expulsion. Criticism of the institution leads to "spiritual counseling" that really amounts to "shape up or ship out." That may seem good on the surface, but it ultimately leads to submission...which includes intellectual acquiescence...and the final product is a student who is not prepared to deal with the real problems that are present in the real world. Four years wasted in an environment that is not real, avoids conflict of any nature, and insulates itself against the realities of professional and personal life.

I am saying all these things in an effort to explain why I'm writing this book. I *know* what a University is and I've been a staff member on two of the finest campuses in the country. Both Iowa State University and the University of Florida have world-wide reputations. Oral Roberts never had *any* university administrative experience before he became "President" of the campus which he built with dollars contributed by thousands of uninformed contributors.

I *have* an *earned* degree from one of the toughest academic institutions in the world. Oral Roberts does not. In other words, my background and experience in university administration should indicate that I know what I'm talking about.

And if God ever told me to do anything, He told me to write this book.

Contents

Chapter 1

The Mechanics
of Big Religion

I Answer Every Letter

"I Answer Every Letter...that comes to me," says Oral Roberts on most of his telecasts. He makes a point of telling his TV audience, usually during his book offer or during the prayer near the end of the telecast, that the mail he receives means a great deal to him. And it does mean a great deal to him, in many ways, but the implication he makes is that he *reads* every letter. And that is *not* the case at all!

For one thing, Oral is only human and there isn't any way he could read all his mail. According to an Oral Roberts executive who keeps tabs on Oral's mail, the mail room at the Oral Roberts Association is capable of handling over 20,000 letters per day. That means opening, sorting, accounting for contributions, and preparing some kind of answer to those 20,000 individuals who write to Oral Roberts everyday. If Oral did read all those letters and did personally provide an answer, he'd have to be a speed reader of the highest order...and then some!

To illustrate the point, let's divide those 20,000 letters received in one day by the number of hours...fourteen...that Oral has said he works everyday. If Oral spent all of those fourteen hours per day just reading his mail...20,000 letters per day...that would mean he would have to be able to read at least 1,428 letters per hour. Now, 1,428 letters per hour break down to 24 letters per minute. Or, to demonstrate it another way, Oral would be reading his mail at the rate of one letter every two seconds. If we give Oral the benefit of the doubt and assume he could answer a letter just as quickly as he could read it, then we could split that two seconds in half and assume that he could read a letter in one second and answer it with the remaining second!

I rather doubt that even Oral's most ardent supporters will believe he could perform such superhuman feats. And, of course, the simple truth is that Oral Roberts *cannot* and *does not* answer his mail...*or read it*...in the manner in which he implies on his television program.

The question then left to be answered is...how *does* he answer all that mail and *who does read it?* When the mail comes into the Oral Roberts Association building, it goes to the mail room and is run through mechanical letter openers. Those opened letters are then separated into two categories: 1) money enclosed or 2) no money enclosed.

The letters coming in from people who write to Oral about their problems are actually read by "letter analysts." Well over one-hundred of them are employed by the Oral Roberts Association. These letter analysts skim through the letters and categorize the problems the writer has revealed about himself. Human problems...at least the kind which people write to Oral Roberts about...are broken down into several categories. While I don't know all of the categories, I do remember some of them: health, finances, marriage, spiritual, family, and faith. There may be other categories, but these are the ones which most people write about when they reveal their problems to Oral.

The letter analysts read the letters and then code them according to types of problems mentioned. The codes assigned to the letters by the analysts are then matched with paragraphs that have been prepared to answer the types of questions asked by most people. These coded letters are then sent to another area where they are "loaded" into a computer system which matches coding with paragraphs written to answer questions about certain types of human needs.

In short, everyone who says they have a financial problem will get the same kind of computerized answer from Oral's computer system. The paragraphs which have been prepared to answer the kinds of questions people ask are changed periodically...but even the changes are not written by Oral personally. The editorial department is generally responsible for preparing new paragraphs on a routine basis. The new paragraphs are mulled over by a couple of vice-presidents, perhaps rewritten or edited somewhat, and *then* they are forwarded to Oral. Oral looks over the paragraphs and may change the wording or the paragraphs may come back down "from the hill" untouched. Generally, he'll make *some* changes so that it can always be demonstrated that he has provided personal input into the preparation of those paragraphs.

The point is: he doesn't really write the paragraphs himself; he merely editorializes someone else's work in order to make it read more like he wants it to read. He has made the statement, "When *I* write something, it's written a certain way." The actual truth is that when he editorializes something which one of his staff members has written for him, he personalizes it. And while that may be legitimate in the eyes of many people, it is not what most people think of when they receive a letter back from Oral after they've written to him. They feel that Oral Roberts personally has read their letter and then answered it. *Not so!*

When I first realized how the mail was answered, I began to have serious doubts about the validity of the methods used. I began to wonder just how far one can go in using present-day technology to answer personal, intimate mail...and still have a ministry based upon integrity, truth, and genuine concerns for the types of needs which people write about to Oral Roberts. By necessity, he has been forced to extend himself with technology available to him. I accept that, and perhaps most people would. Christ extended himself with twelve disciples and Oral has extended himself with a direct mail system, a television program reaching millions, and regional representatives who are trained in estate analysis. But what is the purpose of it all? Is it to help people? Is it all designed to help people improve their lives? Is it all designed to make people happier? Is its purpose to provide fulfillment of basic human needs? Is its purpose to heal? Is it valid?

For a long time, I was not sure I knew the answer to those questions. I am certain of this, however. If people's needs were the primary concern and if Oral had absolutely no misgivings whatsoever about using technology in order to extend his personal ministry into the lives of millions, then there should be no apparent reluctance on his part about revealing the use of such technology. I would think he would want to clarify on national television that he cannot answer all his mail in ordinary ways and that he uses technology for assistance. He could reveal, with absolute confidence about the outcome, that he uses computers to help him; and that while he does not personally read all of those letters that come in, he does personally approve new paragraphs each month dealing with all kinds of personal problems, that his advice is valid and based upon things God has told him to write, and that he then entrusts his employees to choose those paragraphs which match the problems people write to him about. He could then add that he doesn't really sign all those letters, but that a special printing device is used, with special ink, and that his personal signature is duplicated as nearly as possible through the avenues available to him with present-day technology.

He could also use his magazine, "Abundant Life," to reveal the same kind of information about how he uses technology to extend his ministry. And if everything he is doing is something which Oral, himself, considers to be absolutely valid, then there should be no reason why he wouldn't want to do just what is outlined above. I think, however, that there are plenty

4

of reasons why nothing like what I've suggested has ever been done. I think that Oral Roberts is *very* aware of the reasons why people write to him personally. They want *his* personal attention to be given to *their* personal problems. For one thing, his ministry is projected as a very personal one. His ministry, his television program, and his direct mail approach are geared toward people with terrible problems culminating in deep personal needs. When you're dying of cancer, it becomes a very personal thing. You want and expect personal attention from your physicians. You're vulnerable and any treatment you get is going to become more personal than if you had just walked in off the street for a root canal. You *need help personally* and you expect it to come in personal ways from *anyone you may happen to turn to*. And when you turn to Oral, you expect his personal attention!

Oral knows this and he thrives upon projecting an image of personal concern over people's personal problems. If he were to publicly admit to a large segment of his following that his personal attention to his partners has been buffered by layers of present-day technology, it would decimate his audience. *And I think he knows that!*

I Pray Over your Letters

The real eye-opener, however, relating to the manner in which Oral's mail is handled doesn't really have anything to do with how it is answered. What bothers me is the way he uses technology to pray over the letters he receives in the mail. He has, over the years, established a "custom" of taking letters from his partners into the Prayer Tower and praying over them. One of his monthly letters to his partners in 1977 dealt specifically with the "fact" that he took several thousand letters into the Prayer Tower and spent all day praying over them...asking God to meet the needs of the people who had written all those letters. Pictures of him with letters in his hands appeared in "Abundant Life" showing him praying over stacks of letters. The combined campaign relating to that trip into the Prayer Tower with all those letters was designed to raise money…and it was grossly misleading.

"How and why?" you might ask. Very simple. Oral didn't really pray over the actual letters that all those people had mailed to him. Instead, he prayed over computer printouts of several hundred pages that contained only (1) the names of the people who had written to him, and (2) the problem about which they had written. The stacks of printouts were piled up according to categories: finances, health, marriage, etc. It is my contention that this is not what people expect when they write to Oral Roberts and ask him to pray over their problems. I further believe that if they knew this, they wouldn't write, much less send money to him.

Regardless of whether my conclusions are correct about how people might react to the above practice, I can say this: I've read some of the actual letters that came into the reading room, addressed to Oral Roberts. It was obvious from reading the letters that the people writing them thought Oral would give his personal attention to their particular problem. Some of the letters were heartrending. The contents of some of them revealed impending death, broken homes, squalor, and misery. Those people were desperate. Many of the letters expressed a last ditch attitude…"Oral, if your prayers can't help me, I don't have a chance." Reading those letters would make *anyone* want to get down on his knees and pray for the persons who had written them. In other words, reading the contents of many of those letters is a saddening, sobering, and depressing experience.

On the other hand, I have sat in the conference room of the Oral Roberts Association building with stacks of printouts in front of me. They were there to be taken into the Prayer Tower for Oral's prayers. I went down the lists and sat there reading names and categories of problems. Sheet upon sheet upon sheet upon sheet of names on the left side with nothing on the right except "finances" or "health." That activity did not move me emotionally. It did not make me feel sympathy for the person's name on the page. It was impersonal. It was an abstraction. It was an extension of a communication from someone...a communication altered to the point where it was no longer personal. It was nothing more than a name and a problem spit out by a high-speed computer...along with thousands of other names and problems. It was technology, but it had none of the characteristics of a personal ministry. I was appalled. Perhaps I'm too sensitive. Perhaps I'm too critical. Perhaps I'm wrong to think that Oral's use of technology, in this particular manner, is wrong. I'm not sure.

I do feel strongly about this: a ministry that projects itself as having the capability to give your personal problem some personal attention should do just that. Christ did not bring Lazarus back from the dead through some sort of "do not fold, spindle, or mutilate" technology. When Christ healed the blind man, he mixed his own spit into clay and personally placed it onto the blind man's eyes. Christ, in his personal ministry, mingled with the crowds. He did not die on the cross by proxy. And when Christ went out into the desert for forty days and nights, he went there clad in sandals and a sheet, not a $500 Brioni suit! He didn't go to Palm Springs for "R & R" in a million dollar home...as Oral Roberts regularly does! Christ rode on a donkey, not in a $25,000 Mercedes or a Cadillac Seville!

So, what does it all mean? Why is it that Oral's ministry... and nearly any large ministry for that matter...seems to be geared up to handle large amounts of money? Why is there always some new project that needs more money in order to be completed? Why is there always some book to be sold or given away, or some mailing list which is used to solicit funds? What is the purpose of it all? What outside charities or mission endeavors does he support? I've never heard tell of any. The Oral Roberts companies control several banks. I don't hear about him offering loans to Christian businessmen. Instead, it is always one way: "You send the money, I'll send the prayers."

The Volume of It All

One begins to wonder why Christ settled for the Sermon on the Mount. Instead, he could have said something like this: "Give me *your* scraps of food as a token of your faith. Give it to me, and I will pray over it before I partake of it. And when I partake of it, I will pray for you. And we will both expect many, many miracles. Amen and Amen." *Background music up, with lyrics, "and nothing less will do."*

Just what kind of ministry would a modern-day Christ be expected to build if he were to come back and walk this earth today? The first thing he would need to do would be to acquaint himself with the mechanics of a direct mail system that would deliver God the Father, God the Son, and God the Holy Spirit to the masses at bulk rates. Assuming that Christ could pick that up in a very short time, just what kind of cash inflow could he expect...if he wished to be in the same financial league as an Oral Roberts?

As previously stated, Oral's mail room is equipped to handle over 20,000 letters per day. According to one vice-president of the Oral Roberts Companies, ninety percent of those envelopes have money in them. The average gift is $5.00. Now, an average gift of $5.00 isn't very much...unless you're getting 18,000 gifts like that per day. If my arithmetic is correct, that tallies out to a daily income of $90,000.

On a five-day week, that turns into $450,000 per week. Fifty-two weeks a year puts Oral Roberts' non-profit corporate income into the neighborhood of $23,400,000 per year. Actual figures are higher than this and approach $60,000,000 per year!

Ultimately, regardless of which aspect of Oral's ministry one looks at, the path keeps leading toward the same types of questions: Why are things done the way they are? And further, why are things done like that under the aegis of religion? Eventually, as you begin to travel some sort of time path in Oral's life, or theme path within the Oral Roberts' organization, you always end up in an arena that spells "big business."

For example, let's compare Oral Roberts with an average minister who might occasionally be inclined to pray for the sick. Most ministers stay within their churches, within their own denominations, within the parameters which customarily define a "church." The economics of their individual careers, as ministers, are pretty much determined by the economics of the community in which their church exists. In short, their lives, their ministries, and the economics of their existences tend to be community oriented. Religion, which has always been essentially a one-on-one encounter between a sinner and a man of God, has nearly always been limited by the kind of factors enumerated above. As a church becomes larger, additional ministers are hired. Why? To maintain a one-to-one, personal relationship with the congregation.

Upward mobility, the kind that allows people in different walks of life to be promoted within their organization(s), tends to be within some kind of organizational structure. And, it's the same with preachers. If they're good organizers or administrators, they often get promoted out of a church into some kind of regional position...within a district, a diocese, or a synod, etc. But, *always*, it is within some kind of predetermined structure that has been formed by someone *above* them. Now, if you're a man of God who is also a "company" man, that sort of upward mobility is enough to satisfy you. You work within the structure, for the structure, and in turn, the structure rewards you for having done a good job.

If, however, your ego is too big for that type of orderly progress within a predetermined structure, you're going to be mighty unhappy unless you can come up with a vehicle that will let you break away and do your own thing at your own speed. And that kind of ego is the thing that gets at the heart, the essence, and the ambitions of an Oral Roberts. He has

9

always wanted to do things *his* way, run *his* game, run *his* show, according to *his* rules.

Very soon in his career, he became an evangelist. Apparently one church wasn't big enough for Oral Roberts, so he traveled around from church to church, from one meeting hall or auditorium to another. He was on the move; I believe he *had to move*. Why? His ego drove him. That's what I believe.

Oral Roberts has often said that he wanted to be governor of Oklahoma. But, there again, you have to work within a structure...and Oral doesn't want *any* part of *any* structure that he doesn't have some control over, personally. Again, he wants to do things *his* way.

Now, how can anyone do things their way almost totally and be able to get away with it? *Pick religion!* Religion, as a common denominator, has a broader base, a wider appeal, and a greater audience than any other single entity on earth.

If you can get your little snowball rolling down that slope of humanity that responds to religion, you can very soon have yourself a very big snowman in your "front yard." And, if you keep cool, and stay within the right territorial boundaries, no one will ever try to melt your monument. Not very many people, even politicians and bureaucrats, are going to take on religion. Religion, after all, is supposed to be sacred. And that's what makes it such a windfall for a man with the ambitions of an Oral Roberts.

Look, in general terms, at his career as a minister. Look at the central thrust of his appeal. He chose "healing." You'll have to admit, there isn't much competition in that religious "specialty." Also, people are vulnerable where their health is concerned. I've seen people who had never entered a church go to one of Oral's tent meetings...just to let him pray for them. They hoped they'd be healed of their cancer, or their heart condition, or their polio.

In other words, people who have never been "religious" might tend to respond to a ministry that had a component that appealed to a very personal need they felt. As another example of this last ditch survival syndrome, people risk jail to buy laetrile for cancer.

Look at the size of Oral's ministry. Auditoriums, then tent meetings, then direct mail, then television. Oral has, over the years, continually worked toward enlarging his audience. As his audiences became larger, so did the offering plates, so did the contributions, so did his bank accounts. But, as his audiences grew, his personal contact with them decreased. A television audience of 50 million doesn't necessarily put Oral into any closer contact with that person out there who needs to be healed. Can Oral heal anyone on Channel 8? Who knows? But, the numbers are large and that seems to be the intent, the thrust, the direction Oral has always wanted to take.

For years, he avoided firm alliances with denominations that would tie him down to an organizational creed. He used ministerial organizations to help him set up crusades and has maintained informal contacts over the years with various clergymen who might be in a position to help him in the future. But, he remained autonomous and always did *his* things, *his* way, on *his* schedule.

I once asked an Oral Roberts executive what made Oral stop holding tent meetings. The answer blew me right out of the saddle…"air conditioning," the man said! That's probably the only instance where technology put a damper on Oral… rather than him being able to use this new technology it put a damper on his ability to attract people.

If people would no longer continue to come out in the hot summer evenings for a cool hoedown under a huge tent, where would Oral's ministry go? What would he…what could he…do? He had to find another mechanism…something that people would identify with, something that he could incorporate into his ministry of the laying on of hands.

He decided to build himself a "university." Over the years, as the son of a minister, I have noticed that Christians reveal a peculiar wariness about the education of the masses. In general, as the level of education is increased, the tendency to rely upon religion as a source of answers to life's problems becomes less and less important. That bothers clergymen, in general, and people like Oral in particular. He nearly had a fit when his son, Ronnie, went off to Stanford and began running into agnostics and atheists.

Somewhere, within the inner recesses of Oral's mind, it is my speculation that he knew he'd have to hang his ministry on something other than healing and tent meetings one day. Along came air conditioning and the whole thing nearly went up in smoke!

Gradually, the concept of building a "university" that would become his logo, his signature, began to take shape in Oral's mind. And, of course, we all know today that the central visual which Oral usually relies upon to validate himself and his ministry is Oral Roberts University. While the campus is rather garish, it does tend to appeal to the type of people who respond to him. While some people may joke about the fact that his campus looks like "Six Flags Over Jesus," the Prayer Tower in the center is a remarkable piece of psychology in architecture.

The people who had grown up with Oral Roberts now had children who were approaching college age. Naturally, some of them would want to send their kids to Oral Roberts University. Their children could go to ORU and graduate as whole men and women...in body, mind, and spirit. And with that, Oral was off and running again.

He's "respectable" now, he's no longer primarily a faith healer, he's an "educator." He's a "university" president, someone to be reckoned with on a legitimate basis. What is important is this: With the existence of a "university," he has a symbol of respectability to lean upon. It holds him up and allows him to continue in a ministry that is directed toward an ever-increasing audience. Any parent knows that, in addition to his health, he is vulnerable where his children are concerned. If that parent out there is really worried about his kid getting "high" on drugs at UCLA or wherever, he can always send the kid to ORU where he will be educated under the watchful eye of Oral Roberts. If the parent is a typical old Oral Roberts supporter, the chances are pretty high that the parent never went to college himself, so he doesn't really have much of an idea what a college education is actually supposed to be, anyway! The parent sees pretty grounds at ORU, a Prayer Tower, dormitories, a chapel, and hears things about the rigid dress codes and the Honor Code which all students have to live by at Oral Roberts University. As far as that kind of parent can tell, Oral Roberts University is a good, safe place to send the kids.

So the snowball continues to grow. Parents get added to mailing lists, pictures of the campus are used on nearly all of Oral's Sunday morning shows, reaction shots of clean-cut youngsters are used during Oral's sermons...and who is going to be able to criticize any of that?

No one. Unless they've spent over three years working for Oral and found out about some of the inner workings and decided that what was going on was not all that it appeared to be. What I see is a money game...a man running his own show, maintaining his nonprofit status, retaining his autonomy and independence and the capability to do things the way he wants to. What I see is an ego trip that hasn't been fully described...because Oral hasn't yet arrived at his final destiny.

He has never sold one of his books on television. He *gives* them away...and then gets you on his mailing list. Then he'll send you several types of letters until one of them hits one of your "hot buttons"...that is, if you've got a hot button he knows about. And, if you're down in life far enough to write for one of *his* books, you've probably got a hot button that he does know about. And the chances are pretty high that, in time, you'll make some kind of financial commitment to his ministry...even if it's only for five dollars.

The fact that people write in expecting personal attention from Oral...even though they probably won't get it...is not a crime. It isn't illegal and it probably wouldn't even be considered immoral by many people. But, that doesn't necessarily make it right, does it?

Annointing Oil

Finally, in order to illustrate why technology shouldn't be applied to religion, let me relate the circumstances revolving around one of Oral's recent "giveaways"...the vial of annointing oil that he gave away to over 100,000 partners.

Annointing oil has "roots" that go back to Christ, baptism, and christening. It is often used in churches at one time or in one way or another. Whether annointing oil has any real powers or not isn't the question in this case. Annointing oil, as customarily used in most religious circles, is generally olive oil. Christ used olive oil and so did his disciples.

The decision was made to give away annointing oil to Oral's partners as part of a monthly letter that was designed to raise money. George Stovall, Vice-President for Operations of the Oral Roberts Association, was the person usually responsible for handling the details and logistics of a giveaway. The story he related to me was that when he began negotiations to purchase enough olive oil to fill as many as 250,000 vials (complete with fake alabaster holder), he began to run into potential problems with FDA regulations. You see, olive oil is listed by the FDA as basically a food product and Oral Roberts isn't in the food business. For example, if some olive oil were to become rancid and some small child swallowed it and became sick, the Oral Roberts Association could have been held legally responsible. They didn't want any part of that.

At that point, they began looking around for suitable substitutes for olive oil and finally they found one...after sampling and smelling all types of oils that might be acceptable olive oil surrogates. The substitute they settled upon was described to me by George Stovall as "refined hydrocarbons." It was tasteless, odorless, and basically an inert product similar to mineral oil. If some small child were to swallow a vial of it out there in Boone, Iowa, the side effects would be harmless. That was deemed acceptable and they proceeded with plans to fill an initial order of 200,000 vials with the "refined hydrocarbons"...and they would call it annointing oil.

Part of the "power" of the campaign involving the annointing oil was vested in the fact that Oral was supposed to personally pray over the oil and bless it for his partners. That apparently was supposed to make it more effective; ultimately, the question arose, "how would Oral pray for all that annointing oil?" Several options were considered by George Stovall, Ron Smith, and Oral himself. One of the options offered during that conversation suggested that Oral be taken to the holding tank...where-upon he would just lean up against that storage tank and lay hands upon it, and bless all the "refined hydrocarbons" therein! For some reason not ex- plained to me, that suggestion didn't appeal to Oral. Another suggestion offered was that Oral could bless the contents of the tank truck that took the mineral oil from the storage tank to the place where it was then to be poured into the vials. Apparently the image of Oral leaning up against a tank truck, praying for its contents was not something which Oral per- sonally considered viable either. In fact, I gathered the image of him doing that caused a few snickers in the room. In any case, there was some snickering going on between George Stovall and Ron Smith when they told the story to me.

It was suggested that Oral bless the vials of annointing oil after they had been boxed in cartons and ship- ped to the Oral Roberts Association. That was prob- lematic, in that not all of the cartons were to be shipped to Tulsa at the same time. That meant that Oral would have to come back more than once to lay his hands upon cartons of annointing oil vials. Apparently Oral wasn't happy with having to be scheduled into that kind of repetitive activity.

Finally, it was suggested that perhaps he could "symbolically" pray for just a few of the cartons of annointing oil and let the symbolism of Oral's prayers do the job on the rest of the oil. The story I was told was that Oral replied, "Well, if I did that, then the ones I prayed over would be the only ones that actually would work." It is my understanding that no one in the room disagreed with him or snickered at that point.

My point is this: If Oral did, indeed, say that and if he actually felt that a symbolic prayer over just a representative few of those thousands of cartons of annointing oil would be effective over only those which he blessed, then how does he mentally justify praying over a symbolic representation of someone's *real* letter...when by the time he gets it to pray over, it is nothing more than a boiled down list manufactured by that high-speed computer printer?

In other words, when does *real* stop being *real* and become nothing more than an observation of a process that has been altered by technology? When does *real* become phony? When does reality become a charade brought on by utilization of third generation computers?

Is Oral's ministry on television as real as a minister preaching from a pulpit, in a real church, to a real congregation? Is a television prayer by Oral the same as the kind your minister might make when he comes to visit you in the hospital?

When you go to church on Sunday morning and they pass the offering plate, you have a choice of either contributing or not contributing. That's reality. If Oral offers you a book for nothing..."with absolutely no obligation on your part"...and you write in for it and then begin getting letters in the mail which pull at your religious heartstrings and ask for money, is that real, is it valid, is it honest?

When your minister, in church, offers up a prayer during the service for those who are absent, or ill in the hospital, that's real, that's valid, that's honest. When Oral says, "I love your letters, I love to get them. Your letters mean everything to my ministry. I love to pray over them"...and then he

16

actually prays over nothing more than a computerized abstraction of thousands of letters, is that real, is that valid, is that honest?

When your minister in your church gives a sermon that he himself probably spent the better part of a Saturday on, that's real, that's valid, that's honest. When Oral offers to write you back a letter, or give you a book...and neither one of them *was actually written by him,* is that valid, is that honest, is it right?

Chapter 2

The Ultimate Con Game: Capitalizing on III John 2 and other Selected Scriptures

Psychology and Religion

Exactly what is religion and what does it accomplish when it operates in a societal structure? Religion has always tended to be a "unifier," a "normalizer," a "leveler," and has functioned psychologically as a common denominator amongst various segments within society. Because of this, perceptive men down through the ages have always been able to use "God" *and* "country" to appeal to the masses in times of crisis or national emergencies. Politicians and statesmen, in convincing their constituents that God was on their side, have generally been able to mount public opinion and guide it, ride it, toward their goals.

Some of those goals have been worthy and some of them have been justified. I rather doubt that many Americans had any doubts about which side God had to be on when the Japanese bombed Pearl Harbor. Western culture, based upon the tenets of religion and the Golden Rule, had a basis for righteous indignation that resulted in a groundswell of support for retaliation against the Japanese and the German Axis powers. There could be no substantive arguments against such general reactions to the reasons America got itself into World War II. Everything about us, as citizens of a Western culture, made us believe firmly that we had God on our side and that we would ultimately win that war. And, thankfully, we did...for good and just reasons.

There are, however, examples of religion having been used to suppress entire nations, cultures, and civilizations in ways which weren't quite as admirable or as defensible as those which served to justify the United States' entry into World War II. The Germans persecuted the Jews for basically religious reasons. The Crusades during the Middle Ages were based upon religion. And hundreds of thousands were killed in the melee.

Conversely, religion, or the search for religious freedom, has also been used to form nations and nation-states...and religion serves as the underpinnings for the strength today of the Israeli government; the search for religious freedom resulted in the formation of the entire state of Utah; and the Shah of Iran was overthrown because of basic religious principles that millions of Iranians responded to in choosing Khomeini as a figure to rally around.

The above comments are not made with the intent of being critical of religion. Rather, they are intended to point out the power of religion as it relates to the function or dysfunction of a society and its goals. Religion *is* powerful stuff and power is something that can be used for good causes...or it can be used for causes which aren't so good. It all depends upon who's pulling the strings and who's responding when the string-pulling begins.

As an individual with a rather strong Christian upbringing, I have observed myself falling back upon religion when nothing else seemed to be working for me in my life. As a relatively well-educated person with a Christian background, my life-style is basically one in which the Golden Rule is practiced; there are certain moral standards which I observe, and there are certain kinds of things which I would not become involved in...primarily because of Christian beliefs. If everything is going right, however, my life tends to be centered

19

around professional, avocational, and family activities. That's true of most men and women and most families...where jobs, careers, and personal goals provide the primary thrust for a life-style. Religion may serve as a backdrop for many things, but it often takes on a secondary significance as the life-style improves. For example, during good weather, there are many vacant pews in churches around the country that otherwise might be filled with people who are out golfing or going boating on Sunday mornings. In short, religion tends to become less and less important as things improve in our lives, as we become more educated, as our incomes increase, and as our standard of living is elevated to the point where "luxury" becomes something we take for granted.

A natural tragedy, however, such as the untimely death of a child or the demise of a parent tends to bring us all back to the church, back to religion, and back to the source of answers to questions which we begin to ask in times of personal tragedy. In other words, religion has always served to answer questions which education, science, or life-styles could not. The "unknown" has, indeed, always been the realm of religion. We placate ourselves, upon the death of a loved one, with the belief that the spirit of the corpse is happy, warm, and well in heaven. That tends to soothe those of us who remain living and makes it easier for us to resume our lives and our pursuits. We do not wish, as loving humans, to face the possibility that the person going into the ground simply "is not" anymore. We extend that person, our experience with that person, and our love for that person into something perpetual. Since we cannot erase that person from our memories, we perpetuate that person in a way which is more acceptable to us.

And if you, the reader, can separate yourself from your religion long enough to analyze my comments, you'll have to agree that it doesn't matter whether religion is really "true" or not. What is "true" is that it helps you get through times in your life that you cannot handle by yourself. Religion and religious beliefs help us handle the things in our lives *that we cannot handle in any other way.* And if we believe that there really is a God and there really is a heaven, so much the better. I fervently believe they do exist. In other words, my faith and my ability to fall back upon my beliefs, when I need them, helps me to stand and resume my life.

Religion, in the types of circumstances mentioned above, is a stabilizing force in all our lives. And, without it, we would all be much more miserable at certain times if we didn't have it there to lean upon. Religion, then, can be a good thing. *But, it can also be a bad thing.*

Consider, for example, the mass suicides at Jonestown. That was an example of religion at its very worst. What began as a religious experiment turned into something polluted by paranoia, corrupted by megalomania, and the whole thing ended in something which we can only conclude was lunacy.

Religion does not, however, have to be taken to such obvious extremes in order for it to become a negative, rather than a positive, force in our lives. If religion tends to separate us from reality, then it cannot be good. If it does not serve to help us live better lives, then it cannot be good. If it does not serve to make us more productive citizens, then it cannot be good. *Religion can be corrupted!* And religion, if perverted or wrongfully used, can corrupt *us!*

On October 14, 1974, a woman in Bixby, Oklahoma, shot and killed her six-year-old son and her eight-year-old daughter so they "would be close to God." The state psychiatrist, who examined the woman in connection with murder charges brought against her, said, "She had an almost fanatical, pathological thinking about religion that amounted to a spiritual pollution of the mind." The woman was found innocent of first degree murder by reason of insanity in her second trial. After a short time in a mental hospital in Oklahoma, the woman was *released* and subsequently applied for admission to a college...so she could obtain a degree in *criminal psychology* from Northeastern Oklahoma State University.

The college did not wish to accept her as a student and she, in turn, sued the college to force its officials to accept her. To the press, the woman described herself as "wanting to help people in whatever ways God wants me to...physically, emotionally, and spiritually."

Those same words, "physically, mentally, and spiritually," are used to describe the "Whole Man" approach to the education of young men and women at Oral Roberts University! The point is not that Oral Roberts is an ax murderer—he's not that. But a situation like the above illustrates how readily a positive verbal formula can be adopted for use by anyone. Things do go wrong... *even with those individuals who claim to have God on their side!* *its a different between claim + being*

I should make it absolutely clear that Oral Roberts cannot be held responsible for a sick woman who uses words which are widely known to describe the curriculum at Oral Roberts University. Neither can Oral be held responsible in any way for the type of aberration this woman exhibited. She merely was a person who could not handle her life in normal ways and who somehow became so strung out that she twisted the good in religion into something that became bad. She was an extreme example of an aspect of "negative" religion.

Let's look, however, at more acceptable modes of religion. Also, let's examine certain aspects of psychology in religion and make an effort to determine whether the result is positive in a societal sense.

There can be no mistake about whether or not psychology plays a role in the ministry of Oral Roberts. His entire ministry appeals to the psyche of people with terrible needs and it attracts people who are hurting in very real ways.

I once asked Oral's closest associate, "Just how much does Oral know about psychology?" The man replied, *"Everything but what's in the books!"* I countered with another question, "Just what do you mean by that?" He answered, "I mean that he has an innate, uncanny ability to motivate people and that it doesn't matter whether he's read about the psychological basis for motivation or not. He already knows it!"

I queried again, "How?" He merely shrugged and replied, "I don't know. He just does! He has a way with people."

I responded with the remark, "If you put a team of psychologists together to come up with something that would attract people to his ministry, you couldn't pay any amount of money that would produce anything better than *"Something Good Is Going To Happen To You!"*

People Hurting

On every telecast which I helped produce at Oral Roberts University, Oral's Sunday morning shows began with him saying, "Something *Good* is Going to Happen to You." Usually the above phrase was preceded by a statement that tied Oral, himself, into that potentially happy occurrence. For example, Oral would often say something like, "Because *I* know that through *Seed-Faith* you can rise above your problems, Something Good is Going to Happen to You!" He'd often point directly into the camera, at the home viewer, and emphasize the word *Good*. The background music would swell up and the lyrics "Something Good is Going to Happen to You" followed mellifluously and helped set the tone for Richard Roberts' (Oral's son) voice-over which then accompanied shots of the campus and the Prayer Tower. Since I was asked to write the copy for Richard's voice-over during this segment, it was made clear to me that the following copy points were to be emphasized: (1) no matter how big your problems, (2) no matter how bad you're hurting, (3) no matter how hopeless it seems, (4) there is a place called Oral Roberts University, (5) with a Prayer Tower at its very center, (6) there is a man who cares about your problems, (7) there is a man who wants you to be in good health and succeed, and (8) God is always present at the point of your need.

This segment (designed to make a person who had problems respond to the upcoming telecast) *always* ended with, "...and now, author, educator, and evangelist...*Oral Roberts!*" In other words, the copy at the beginning of each show was intended to appeal to people who had real problems in their personal lives...sometimes to the point of getting into specific problems such as finances, health, marriages, broken homes, etc...and grab their attention so they would immediately be able to identify with the kinds of problems being mentioned, and *then* immediately Oral would walk out onto the set to applause, adulation, and the closing lyrics of the song: "Jesus of Nazareth is passing...passing your way!"

When Oral walked out onto that set with that kind of psychological build-up, it was always a goose-bumpy kind of thing. The audience was primed to listen to this man, Oral Roberts, who apparently understood their problems, who had the answers to their problems, and who wanted to help them rise above their problems. The closing lyrics of the song also put Oral very close psychologically to the deity, "Jesus of Nazareth." By design?

Let me recap for just an instant to make it clear: the typical profile of an Oral Roberts supporter is a person who has terrible personal problems. Those problems are usually bad health, a bad marriage, a bad financial situation, or a bad relationship with *someone* or *something*. A person who has those kinds of problems is obviously going to be looking for solutions. Chances are that person is going to experience some kind of emotional catharsis in either solving his problems or being taken under by them. That person is looking for a way out! *And, now, from what this man, Oral Roberts, is saying, it looks like he might have some answers!* That viewer is going to sit there in front of his set at home and watch what comes next, once he is in that frame of mind.

One familiar and important segment of Oral's Sunday morning telecasts is called "the offer." The "offer," in nearly all cases, involves Oral Roberts personally offering to give you, the viewer, a free book "without any obligation on your part" that will "turn your life around." Specifically, the "offer" is designed to appeal to a viewer who has some kind of need. Often, Oral will get into a specific type of problem that his book "covers." He'll get specific about financial problems, for example, and use generic phrases like "I know how low you feel when you can't pay your bills. I've been there." And then Oral will continue to make statements to the effect that his book will help you do things that will help you pay your bills, get that new job, or get that busines of yours back on its feet.

Seed-Faith

Once you write for that book, you're then on his mailing list...and you'll begin getting letters which will attempt to make you become convinced that the way out of your problems is to begin by doing something that requires faith on your part. This is where the concept, *Seed-Faith*, enters into the correspondence and is designed to lead the "participant" to believe that his miracles will begin happening sooner if he contributes to *something*. *Seed-Faith*, as a psychological concept, is based upon one principle: give independently from your need, and expect a miracle back from God. What you are expected to give, through implication, is money. While *Seed-Faith*, as a concept, indicates that you can give time, talents, or money to anyone (not necessarily Oral Roberts), the subtleties of the copy point toward giving to Oral Roberts. For one thing, his books generally contain examples of people who gave him money and *then* got their miracles. Never have I read, in any of Oral's books, where he advised you to expect your miracle and then give something as a payment back to God in return for the miracle. *You give first*, his books advise, *and then expect miracles in your life*.

Oral's closest associate once told me, "*Seed-Faith* put Oral's ministry back on the map." When he said that, he was talking about both the concept and the book which Oral wrote by that same title. To reiterate, the concept of Seed-Faith is simple: You have to give something; give it because you have a need that you want to be met, and then you have to expect a miracle back from God. The obvious suggestion is (through several examples in Oral's books) that you should give money. It is further implied that you should give it to Oral Roberts. He'll pray with you for your miracle!

He gives one example, in the book *Seed-Faith*, about the farmer who saved his best corn for seed. The farmer put his best corn back into the ground as seed. What follows next is commentary to the effect that faith is a seed you plant. Faith begins by doing something. And what you should do is give something...perhaps money...as a sort of conceptual seed in order to get back a crop of miracles that will turn your life and all your problems completely around!

Have you ever gotten one of those sweepstakes letters in the mail, where it is indicated that several hundred thousand dollars are going to be given away to some lucky person...regardless of whether they (you) order any magazines or not? You never get a notice in the mail about the sweepstakes or the giveaway that doesn't, at the same time, give you an opportunity to order the magazines they have for sale. You get the total package at the same time: "We're going to give lots of money away, and while it doesn't matter whether you order magazines or not, you have a chance to win all this money and you can order now too!" If it really didn't matter to anybody (the reader of his mail *or* to the sweepstakes people) you feasibly could get separate mailings: one would inform you of the giveaway and another separate mailing (that didn't mention the giveaway) would appeal to you to order magazines. But, it doesn't work that way.

I've always toyed with the thought, even though I know it isn't true, that I might have a better chance of winning that hundred thousand dollars if I just ordered one magazine. Now, those campaigns are honest. They do, in fact, give away thousands of dollars, and they also help to sell thousands of magazines. Quite obvious to any businessman is the conclusion that the giveaways would not be continued if they weren't financially successful...and served to sell magazines at a profit which exceeds the amount of dollars given away. We all know *that* as well as we know the sun will come up in the east. Right? But, if our subscription to a particular magazine is about to run out, or there's a magazine that we're the least bit interested in, we go ahead and order it...just in case. *It might make a difference.* And whether it does or not, we get back a publication that's usually offered at the going rates...or perhaps with a little shaved off the regular newsstand price. In any case, we get back value received for the money we send in.

What about an appeal, though, that pulls at my fear that I am going to die of this cancer that I have. The doctors have told me it's hopeless and just a matter of time. I'll start grasping for straws like you or any other human would who has an instinct for survival. I may try to obtain Laetrile. I may watch Oral Roberts television show and write for his book. I may read his book and begin to think that perhaps if I send him money *out of my need*, that perhaps I'll be miraculously healed of my cancer.

The psychology works. Oral gives millions of books away "at absolutely no obligation" and his mail is full of letters from people who write in after having read the book(s), have sent in money, and are now expecting, *bless God*, a mind-boggling miracle to hit them any day!

The psychology is remarkably similar to the "Dare to be Great" principle. And it does work (for Oral), because he gives books away from *his* need and gets back money in return! *It works!*

It works. And it works so well for Oral Roberts that he's built a campus with the money that has come in from other believers. How could anyone in their right mind argue that the concept of *Seed-Faith* doesn't work?

Let's consider, now, a typical article which has appeared in Oral's magazine, "Abundant Life," which illustrates how

Seed-Faith works for those who decide to participate in the concept. The example follows: A photo was shown of a couple who wrote a letter stating that their financial situation had been in a mess, because the husband was out of work. They sent in their *Seed-Faith* gift, began poring over the want ads, the husband applied for several jobs, and finally landed one. *Bless God, their miracle had come through! They could now pay their bills!*

I just wonder if that couple could have gotten their finances straightened out simply by poring over those want ads and applying for jobs...without ever having given anything to Oral. Could that be possible? Lots of people with financial problems write to Oral and send him money, apply for jobs and then get them, so it probably wouldn't work if all they did was apply for those jobs. Right?

III John 2

There is, however, more to the psychology of Oral's ministry than just *Seed-Faith*. He goes to the scriptures and finds the ones that corroborate or support his concepts. One scripture which both Oral and Evelyn have said is their favorite is III John 2. It reads, "Beloved, I wish above all things that thou mayest prosper and be in good health, even as thy soul prospereth."

That scripture, according to Oral Roberts, means that God wants you to succeed (financially), and wants you to be in good health. The only provision that accompanies that divine wish is that your soul must also prosper.

Now, most ministers and most religions have one thing in common: the basic message inherent in most sermons is that man was born in sin and that he must make up for that by his faith in God. Hellfire and brimstone are often integrated into such doctrines. In other words, you'll go to Hell if you ͏don't fall down on your knees and repent your sins. Within the of environment, a sense of guilt nearly always precedes an emotional capitulation to the validity of religion in your life. You have to accept your original sin (being born); repent of any transgressions you've been guilty of; promise to obey God and then try and walk the "straight and narrow." Those are hard rules to live by and that's what kept the confessionals so busy within the Catholic Church for so many years! Further, the "straight and narrow" is a difficult row to hoe and it doesn't tend to wear very well in the long run. It's too difficult. Can you really enjoy your life when those kinds of restrictions are placed upon your fun?

Oral avoids that kind of trap and it has served to increase his audience. He tells people, "God is a good God." "God wants you to prosper and be in good health." The part about your soul prospering is de-emphasized and is subtly pointed toward *Seed-Faith*. He doesn't say that in order for your soul to prosper you must walk the straight and narrow. He says that, in order for your soul to prosper you must give God your best and then expect His best back in return. Usually, when you give God your best, it means giving money...*give God your biggest bill, not your smallest. Give God your best and expect back a whopping miracle in return.* Now, if you're a viewer out there in televisionland and you have some kind of terrible problem that you haven't been able to solve on your own, you're a prime candidate for that type of appeal. If you're desperately down on your luck, in very poor health, or have a marriage that you'd like to see begin working, you'll very likely respond to Oral's message.

You'll write to Oral Roberts for his book. You'll see the "logic" of what he calls *Seed-Faith*. You may just, indeed, give God your best via Oral Roberts and then sit there expecting that miracle you so desperately desire.

What you've done is order that magazine...just to increase your chances of winning the hundred thousand dollars sweep-stakes prize. Both appeals are based upon similar psychological appeals and both are designed to persuade you to "buy the product," to increase your chances of "winning." You, the reader, are free to disagree with me. Take it from me, though, as the guy who was hired to write some of those appeals, what I'm telling you is true and, right now, you're reading from the horse's mouth. I, myself, bought the concept for a while. And then I began to learn about the million dollar homes in Palm Springs, wonder about the $500 Brioni suits, and the $25,000 automobiles. I always understood the psychological effects of the appeals used, and for a while I did believe that there was some validity behind them.

But, when I began to observe that all too many contributors were low-income people, or persons on social security, or individuals with health problems that were beyond the scope of Oral's powers, I found it difficult to justify the high scale of living that Oral enjoys. He surrounds himself with luxury and rather deliberately insulates himself from the kind of people who respond to him in the mail. When he does mix with the people who support him, it is under controlled circumstances *on his turf*. And that is what a "seminar" is all about on the Oral Roberts University campus.

The Seminars

The word "Seminar" as defined by Webster's New Collegiate Dictionary follows: "A group of students (usually graduate) engaged, under a professor, in original research; also the course of study, or the room of meeting." From my own experience as a graduate student at one time, the word seminar was nearly always attached to advanced study under the general guidance of a high-ranking professor. The word "seminar" was never used in a manner which would imply fund raising was involved.

But Oral's definition? Well, in all the time I've worked for him, I've never seen one seminar program that wasn't explicitly tied to a need for money.

People who have previously supported Oral Roberts through his direct mail campaigns are invited to attend a seminar on the Oral Roberts University campus. All you have to do in order to be a seminar participant is *get there*...to the campus of Oral Roberts University in Tulsa, Oklahoma. Once you arrive, everything you do is programmed. You're put up in hotels or dormitories at Oral's expense. Three meals a day are fed to you in Mabee Center...and from a Thursday noon until the following Sunday afternoon, you get "the treatment."

It is group or mass psychology at its very finest! You, as a seminar participant, are soothed with music sung by Richard and Patti (before their divorce), the World Action Singers, and other student groups that are there to demonstrate "the clean-cut look."

Oral preaches to the seminar guests and his sermons lay the groundwork for *Seed-Faith*. The subject of the seminars *is*, in fact, *Seed-Faith*...and I suppose you could conclude that one of his seminars is a graduate level course in how to give your money away and like it!

From the time you arrive, your mind is bombarded with the principles of *Seed-Faith*: give away from your need, give God your best and expect back His best. If you need a big miracle, you have to give big in order to get it back big. You plant a seed and expect a harvest. When you put your nets down into the water, you expect to bring them up filled with fish. You should expect enough fish in that net to sink your boat! Whenever possible, Biblical references are used that tie in with Oral's concept of Seed-Faith. Oral even attributes the practice of *Seed-Faith* to God, Himself, in the following manner: God gave His only son...and therefore His best...to the world in order that God, Himself, would get back a harvest of saved souls. In other words, God planted a seed of faith by giving up His only son to die on the cross...and the harvest back, to God Himself, was the redemption of all who believed.

Throughout these seminars, examples are given of people who have "had their lives turned around" by practicing *Seed-Faith*. You soon begin to get the message that if you really

31

want to get your life into high gear and accomplish everything you've ever dreamed of, you probably ought to give *somebody something*! At various times, throughout the seminar, Oral hints that before you leave Tulsa, you're going to have an opportunity to put your faith to the test and actually have a chance to practice *Seed-Faith*. Any professional salesmen who were to attend one of Oral's seminars would immediately recognize several "trial closes" during the course of the activity. One of Oral's tactics is a mild form of an insult. For example, he'll be talking about *Seed-Faith* and its merits and then make this kind of statement, "and if you've got the nerve to try *Seed-Faith*...if you're man enough, or woman enough... you'll get the opportunity to try it out right here. Right here in this very auditorium. I'm going to test you. You'll be given an opportunity to give God your best. If you don't have the courage to test your faith, that's *your* problem. But, I'll tell you this: If you didn't have a problem that you couldn't use *Seed-Faith* on, you wouldn't be here. *I know why you're here!* You're here because you want a miracle in your life. And, if you want the best miracle you've ever seen in your life, you'd better be prepared to give God your best. And, if you don't have the nerve for it, that's your problem. I just don't want anyone to give one dime if they're not expecting a miracle back in return. I'll tell you this, no one here owes *me* one dime. You go ahead and eat that food I'm feeding you. You go ahead and stay in that hotel room I'm puttin' you up in. That's on me, that's not on God. That's *my* gift. This whole university is *my* gift to God. This may be called Oral Roberts University, but it isn't my university. It's *God's* university. If you don't want to be a part of it, that's fine with me. You can just go on back home and keep on muddlin' around the way you've always done."

And then he'll chuckle. And then the majority of the crowd will begin chuckling. *Group psychology, peer group persuasion.* And the message is very clear: If you want a miracle in *your* life, you'll be expected to give God your *best* before you leave the campus of Oral Roberts University.

And then Saturday morning comes around and the entire seminar audience, usually comprised of about 2,500 people, is given an opportunity to participate in a "project." The projects offered to the seminar guests are usually of the following nature: buildings, dormitories, equipment, air-conditioning systems, married housing units, etc.

These projects are broken down into various price categories that allow the participants to make pledges that might fit into their budgets. Seminars I was familiar with had pledge categories that began as high as $150,000. Usually there were only two or three pledge categories that high. Then the pledge categories went on down the scale to $100,000, $50,000, $25,000, $15,000, $12,500, $10,000, $7500, $5000, $2500, $2000, $1500, $1000, $750, $500, $250. Seldom were there ever any categories below $250. The majority of the gifts were from $15,000 on down.

Generally, the "take" on one of these seminars would be in the neighborhood of $1.5 to $3 million. Nearly always, checks and cash totaled out to approximately three-quarters of a million dollars, with the remainder being made up of pledges that would be paid to the Oral Roberts Association over a certain period of time. Often, after a seminar, I'd ask an Oral Roberts Vice-President, "How'd the seminar go?" He'd reply, "Not bad, two and a half million." Or, he'd give some other equally impressive figure.

In any event, the relative success of a seminar was measured in terms of the total dollars received. At least that's what would be discussed in the next few days following one of these events.

Finally, a seminar would always end on Sunday morning with one whale of a moving sermon by Oral...and then they'd form the healing line. Everyone in the seminar audience got a chance to walk through the line and have Oral Roberts touch them. I don't think I ever saw any of the participants just sit up in the auditorium and not go down and let Oral touch them. Usually, during a seminar, there were participants who were in wheelchairs. I never saw anyone healed of *anything* and that bothered me. I saw people who had come expecting a healing and I saw the raw hope and desire in their eyes. If faith *could* have brought them up out of those wheelchairs, they would have come *out* and been ready to run a 50-yard dash, on the spot! It *never* happened.

Oh, once in a while someone would get up out of a wheelchair and limp off the stage. But, I'd seen them a day or two before get out of their wheelchairs to get into cars or go into the restroom. They weren't total and incurable wheelchair cases. They merely needed the wheelchairs for comfort because of the particular illness they had. They *could*, however, get up and walk short distances if they *had* to, or if they *really wanted to*. They really wanted to for Oral, so they'd do it and then return to their wheelchairs backstage. It was a dog and pony show!

I never, on a Monday morning after a seminar, ever heard *one* person in the organization talk about how many people were healed during a seminar. The only figures I *ever* heard relating to seminars were dollar figures!

Didn't someone once say, "There's a sinner born every minute." Well, for all of those sinners out there who are looking for some kind of emotional catharsis that will get them off their back-slidin' ways, there is always a seminar to get them moving and grooving on God. There are generally six to nine such seminars every year at Oral Roberts University, and according to my rough arithmetic, that totals out to a dollar intake in the neighborhood of $15 to $25 million per year...by using $2.5 million as an average take on a seminar. That's not bad! And it does help finance those buildings, equip those classrooms, and build dormitories, married housing units, and medical school facilities. *And all on God's university!*

Why none of it really helps people

The manner in which Oral Roberts' management team rationalizes a seminar is rather peculiar. One of Oral's top associates readily admits that while no one is ever healed of a physical problem at a seminar, the content of the seminar "touches" the lives of the participants and makes them better people, providing a catharsis of religious emotions which spurs them onto bigger and better things in life. In other words, the effect of a seminar is supposed to be, by their definition, a mental and/or spiritual experience which results in an improved approach to life.

A salesman's pep rally does that, too. So does a Positive Thinking Rally. The charge for attendance at a Positive Thinking Rally is $10...at least that's what it was in 1977 when I produced one on videotape with Art Linkletter, Earl Nightingale, and Paul Harvey, et al. Those types of rallies, however, are short-lived in their effect. Ask any sales manager and he'll tell you exactly that. Even the best of sales forces needs its positive thinking juices revved up on a rather regular and routine basis. Very few salesmen are ever left on their own for long without some kind of mental programming being provided by the company...in order to keep that salesman thinking positively out there as he calls on one customer after another. "Positive reinforcement" is what the psychologists call it. Salesmen call it getting a shot in the arm. It's a virtual necessity with any sales force that is out there getting hit with "no" answers at least half of the time. "Positive Thinking Rallies" help salesmen rationalize the "no" answers while, at the same time, making their mental best of the "yes" answers.

What about that poor guy out there, though, who makes his contribution to Oral Roberts and then sits back waiting for his miracle to jump up and hit him right in the middle of his unsatisfactory life? There are, in fact, people out there in the real world who simply aren't capable of ever becoming the president of their company. They never will become

35

millionaires or even experience moderate success in developing an estate of any kind. Sad as it may be, there are people out there in our world who are losers. They have to be. For one thing, not everyone can be a winner...someone *has* to lose in any game. And that includes the game of life, if you'll excuse the expression.

Faced with that reality, how can any organization justify its existence when, in effect, the improbable desires of an incapable multitude are exploited. Is it possible that the members of such an organization really believe that what they're doing is valid? And, if so, why do they become so defensive if their motives are questioned? Further, why does one become suspect if he asks such questions? I asked such questions with an open mind and I quickly realized that those were *not* the type of questions which "friendly" employees were expected to ask. While I probably qualified as one of the fortunate few who were "insiders" within the organization, I was given a rather veiled warning, "You're either for us or you're against us. Anything else is rhetoric."

What does a statement like that mean? I've concluded that it means you either wholeheartedly support *all* activities, *or* keep your discreet mouth shut, *or* you leave the organization.

While the success of a seminar, for instance, might be hinged upon the amount of money brought in, the general tone or an employee's reactions...once he's been admitted into such a conversation about a seminar...had better be positive, filled with team spirit, and completely devoid of any uncertainties about validity, value received, or intrinsic worth of such "programs."

Since I was primarily in television, perhaps they expected that I'd be just a bit "different" and made allowances for my attitudes...and went ahead and shared information with me, thinking I'd come around. I'm sure when they read this book, they'll wish they hadn't discussed as much with me as they did.

Therefore, *it is important* that you, the reader, understand that I was not initially critical of *any* activities I viewed at Oral

Roberts University. To the contrary, I was initially impressed with nearly everything that occurred. They tend to do things on a grand scale at ORU. Further, when they decide to do something, they go after it with alacrity. I liked that! In general, I'm a bit impatient and I enjoy moving ahead rapidly on priority projects...and since television programs ranked very high on the list of priorities at ORU, I seldom ran into any obstacles that a good bit of persuasive logic couldn't overcome.

Increasing doubts, however, began to creep into my mind as I became more and more a participant in planning sessions, management discussions, and was then given an opportunity to contribute to the creative substance of various "campaigns." It became increasingly evident, as a result of those activities, that there was a great deal of attention being given to psychological motivators, "hot buttons," and universal emotional appeals. In another manner of speaking, those "campaigns" weren't inspired by God at all, they were contrived by men...using all the tools one would expect to find within an advertising agency on Madison Avenue. That disturbed and annoyed me. Oh, I'd used those tools before on "up front" fund-raising campaigns at other universities, but I'd never used them "for God."

If those members of top management within the Oral Roberts "companies" were inspired by God, they certainly wouldn't have had to waste their time worrying about whether or not a seminar brought in the desired amount of money. Or, more appropriately, they wouldn't have made such a point of actually bragging about how much money was brought in. My faith in the organization began to show a few hairline cracks.

The dead baby

What really busted up my beliefs in the integrity of the organization, however, stemmed from an incident which involved one of the faculty members of Oral Roberts University.

37

He and his wife had a young baby who became ill. This particular faculty member apparently decided to really put the power of prayer to the test and began praying for the child rather than taking it to a hospital. The baby's illness became more and more severe until the infant actually died right in the home of the faculty member.

That, in itself, is sad enough. But, the story gets worse. The couple then decided to begin praying and fasting to bring the infant back to life. In addition, they requested that Oral come into their home and also pray for the child. The words used by a certain ORU Vice-President to describe Oral's reaction to that request were, "He wouldn't touch that with a ten-foot pole. That dead baby was in their home (the faculty couple's home) for three days before I could get a doctor in there and get that baby out of the house. A story like that would ruin Oral. The press would crucify him."

What shocked me was the description the man gave of Oral's reactions to the incident. Oral Roberts has *always* been a faith-healer. His *entire ministry* has been built around praying for the sick. Christ brought Lazarus back from the dead after he'd been "gone" for three days. If Oral Roberts had had any genuine beliefs in either his *or* God's powers to heal the sick or raise the dead, he'd have recognized that incident as the ultimate opportunity for him to test his beliefs. More appropriately, if he *really* believed in the power of prayer, there is simply *no way* that he would have refused to at least pray for that dead infant.

What did the Vice-President say? He said, "Oral wouldn't touch that with a ten-foot pole." Oral wouldn't go *near* that faculty member's home. He had one of his trusted associates take care of the problem for him, so he, Oral Roberts, wouldn't personally have to get involved in something so potentially scandalous.

As the saying goes, "That blew my mind." I pondered the way the incident was described to me. I pondered Oral's reactions...the way they were described to me. Further, I pondered the possibility that Oral Roberts was simply one human who might have desperately wished that the power of prayer could, indeed, bring a dead infant back to life...but knew that it couldn't. And knowing that, I'm sure he must have known then that the power of prayer simply does not work for Oral Roberts in the manner he's always preached that it does.

Considering all this, I am led to the conclusion that Oral Roberts' ministry of the laying-on-of-hands crumbled in failure *on the day that he refused to go pray for the dead baby.* How else can you look at it?

I have heard Oral say several times that he always tried to obey his parents and obey God. Further, he has said several times that his mother gave him instructions, "Be different, Oral. Be like Jesus."

Jesus prayed for Lazarus and brought him back from the dead. Oral could not bring himself to enter the child's home to pray for the dead baby.

I don't blame him. I couldn't have done it, either. In fact, I don't know of anyone who could. Still, Oral has said that God has told him to "Take My healing power to your generation." God was also to have told him (*Abundant Life,* August 1976, page 16) not to be like other men but be like Jesus and heal people *As He Did.*" This certainly makes him responsible to heal the majority of those to whom he promises healing.

I, personally, have never been blessed or privileged by any audible communication from God. In fact, even though I believe in God, I don't have a memory of God ever having spoken to me in any way. If God ever *had* spoken to me and *had* told me to take his healing power to my generation, I'd have gone into that home and prayed for that baby, dead or not.

Chapter 3

Seven Great Secrets
to Success in Religion

What is it that makes one evangelist a booming success while others with many similarities are seldom heard of? As a child growing up in my father's church, I observed many evangelists, including Oral Roberts, hold revival meetings of one sort or another...and many of them prayed for the sick, delivered resounding sermons about the evils of the devil and the reward waiting in Heaven for those who only believed. Today, none of them are known very well at all and certainly none of them would cause the ripples on the Richter scale the way Oral Roberts has.

One reason for Oral's success is that a smattering of numerology has always been quietly present in his ministry and the number "seven" has figured prominently. He has seven great secrets for his success and he has used them continually over the years.

I. Oral Roberts: a volume dealer

Any good businessman knows that there is an inverse correlation between profit margin and volume. A furniture store, for example, with occasional sales and a high inventory of goods on its floor must mark its merchandise up three to four times above cost. If the furniture store is going to enjoy cash flow, profits that will provide a living for the store owner, and provide working capital for expansion of inventory or facilities, then that kind of markup is an operational necessity.

On the other hand, a grocery store sells food to hundreds of customers each day and it can survive on volume sales at a much lower markup than the store selling furniture.

New car dealers, in analyzing the market in which *their* business will operate, often face the decision of becoming a volume dealer...through heavy advertising, selling lots of cars at lower prices than their competition...or selling their cars at sticker price and doing only a nominal amount of advertising. In the latter category, such a dealership will often rely upon walk-in traffic almost exclusively. In either case, the owner of such a dealership makes a calculated choice of which method he will use in marketing automobiles.

Having bought cars from both types of dealerships, it has been my observation that the high volume, low margin dealer is geared toward sales rather than service. As long as your car runs properly, you're happy with the relatively lower price you paid for your car. However, if your car begins to need service work, you find that the volume dealer often doesn't have the facilities or the inclination to do service work very well or provide follow-up adjustments which might be included under the new car warranty.

The low volume, higher margin dealer, however, wants and needs to be able to provide continual service (including warranty work) on the cars he sells. He wants his customers happy over an extended period of time and his entire approach to doing business is slanted in that direction. In other words, while you might pay a little more for your car when you buy it from a low volume dealer, you'll probably be happier in the long run once your car begins to need servicing.

Most churches which operate within a community, serving local needs of local Christians, are unable to work on volume levels. The size of the congregation of a local church is almost totally predetermined by the size of the community it serves. Therefore, a volume ministry simply is not possible. Such churches provide the typical example of Christian involvement between pastor and congregation and are the backbone of American religion in operation. In the long run, as spiritual needs are experienced...christenings, marriages, deaths in the family...the community church (working on low volume and good service) provides the best "delivery" to a Christian population. The minister of such a typical, community-oriented church is generally a "good guy" who keeps involved in community affairs, may become involved in United Way campaigns, visits church members when they're in the hospital and is available to console members of a family who have lost a loved one.

Most clear thinking Christians patronize such churches... and they have a wide range of sizes, styles, and denominations from which to choose.

There is another level of "religious delivery" that has operated for decades within this country, however, and it has all the characteristics of the volume dealership. With the advent of religious programming on television, the church has been artificially extended into our homes on Sunday mornings. If you're ill and unable to attend church, you can turn on your TV set and watch a host of religious shows on Sunday morning. The audience of such religious shows, instead of being comprised of people within one community, will number in the thousands. Recent figures indicate that as many as 7 million Americans watch religious programming on Sunday mornings from 7:00 a.m. to noon. That's a pretty good-sized congregation.

Such volume dealerships in religion don't often ask you to tithe ten percent of your income to their ministry. Instead, they'll offer to either sell or give you a book "that will turn your life around" and make you a happy, contented, successful Christian. Generally, if you decide to take advantage of such an offer from a volume dealer, you'll also end up on his mailing list and begin getting all sorts of appeals in the mail...asking you to contribute in this or that manner to his ministry.

Everything such a "minister" offers through his mail appeals is based upon volume. When the numbers are high enough, even though the percentage of returns may be rather low, the contributions which come into a volume dealer add up to millions of dollars. As far back as 1955, Oral Roberts' organization was taking in $3 million per year through the mails.

In 1977, that figure was above $30 million and had been in the range between $20-30 million all through the seventies. Oral's televised Sunday morning shows generally air on 150 stations throughout the country in every major market. On every show, in addition to his sermon, he offers to give away a book "with no obligation on your part" *except that you will end up on his mailing lists.* Nearly 20,000 people per day, on an average, will respond to one of Oral Roberts' offers and eventually write in to him for advice...with money enclosed.

Now that's a volume dealership in religion. The person who "buys" from him, however, is going to get the short end of the stick eventually. Sooner or later, that "buyer" is going to need service work! Someone is going to die in the family; someone will need to be visited in the hospital or a pastor will be needed to preside over a funeral. Oral Roberts isn't going to be there. And neither will Rex Humbard, Billy Graham, Reverend Ike, Robert Schuler, or Tony and Susan Alamo. In fact, none of the volume dealers will be there to help you when you need spiritual service work done on your life at a personal level.

The sad thing about such programming, above and beyond the fact that it exists at all, is that the responsibility for such programming falls upon the local television station in your community. The FCC dictates that all television stations must

43

provide a certain amount of public affairs programming which is designed to meet the needs of the community in which it operates. Originally, local religious programming was allowed to be counted as community affairs programming and that eventually led toward the growth of big religion on television.

Generally, a local church cannot afford to extend its ministry via television. A local church which aired its Sunday morning services on television would merely be reaching a local audience. The costs are rather high...as much as $3,000 per hour even on a Sunday morning...and not many local churches can afford to take such risks with their budgets.

That reluctance on the part of local churches leaves a gap on Sunday mornings which local television stations fill with "paid religion" shows of a national nature...such as "Oral Roberts and You." Oral Roberts *does pay* that kind of money to appear on your local television station and the station enjoys an income on Sunday morning that it probably wouldn't otherwise obtain. In some cases, local television stations have endeavored to actually give free air time to local churches, but the economics of that kind of activity have been undesirable. If local church programming were *not* available, TV stations would then air cartoons or local public affairs programming that *would* draw advertisers. In any case, the TV stations in airing such "paid religion" programs meet FCC requirements and are able to keep their licenses.

The real truths of television programming, however, point toward the conclusion that local TV stations *could* afford to give free time on a rotating basis to local churches and *really* provide community affairs programming *at a local level*.

The entire industry would be much more honest about meeting FCC requirements if it did, indeed, begin such practices. The best thing that could happen to Sunday morning programming would be for the FCC to *require* that a portion of time be either sold or given freely to local churches so they could compete with the volume dealers in religion and clear the path for local church programming designed to meet local needs...and also provide follow-up on service work!

Oral Roberts has, in the past, maintained counsel in Washington, D.C., to ward off such a potential catastrophe to his ministry. It is important to the religious volume dealers that such a policy doesn't go into effect. Oral Roberts' Sunday morning audience runs in the vicinity of 2-4 million viewers. On his prime time specials...where he pays local TV stations more money than even the *networks* do for airing *their* programming...his audiences may run above 50 million viewers. On one such Christmas show which had H. R. Puf'N'Stuff and Sigmund the Sea Monster as guests (along with Andrae Crouch) the audience, including Canadian viewers, was calculated to be nearly 63 million. Oral paid $40,000 to Sid and Marty Krofft Productions that Christmas for the appearance of H. R. Puf'N'Stuff and Sigmund...but the take in the mail was worth it!

You, the reader, have a choice to make. You probably have some interest in religion or you wouldn't be reading this book...and you *will* be a religious "customer" at some point in your life. You can get your religion from a volume dealer, get a free book "at absolutely no obligation on your part," get on Oral's mailing list and, perhaps, eventually send him as little as ten dollars after you've read about the miracles of Seed-Faith. Or, for a little more money, perhaps as much as 10% of your income (that's called tithing, remember)...you can get up off your broadening fanny on Sunday morning and go to a local church and involve yourself in a form of Christianity that includes personal attention to your needs. True, you can't go into a local church dressed in pajamas, you'll probably have to put on a suit of good clothes, and have your hair combed. Someone might even ask you to teach a Sunday School class, you might be asked to bring a potluck dish to a church picnic, and you might even be asked to sing in the church choir. Religion, after all, is a two-way street. If you're going to practice Christianity, the day will come when someone will need *your* help in a personal way. Give it to a local church with real people. Avoid the volume dealers in religion who only want to see you in front of the TV sets. In the long run, you'll be much better off.

II. Oral Roberts: being different

No voter is happy with his choice on election day if the differences between candidates for office are unclear. We like to go to the polls and feel secure in the knowledge that we understand the differences between candidates and made a choice that we felt would best serve our individual needs as members of the electorate. The bright, new candidate who comes along for public office and presents a different image than everyone else generally gets the most votes. John F. Kennedy was the best example of this. He absolutely mesmerized the American voters. And whether you liked him or not, when he went into office, he did deliver. He also paid the ultimate price and will, perhaps, go down in history as the most productive and colorful president who ever occupied the White House.

Successful evangelists also strive to be different from others who are competing for attention from a religious electorate. Oral Roberts has *always* endeavored to be somewhat different than other evangelists. He has made the statement, "Not many preachers would have the guts to start a faith-healing ministry." He knew when he started his ministry that it took a lot of nerve to lay hands on the sick. If you don't think so, you get up in front of a large audience and pray for some sick person. It takes nerve! And Oral has a lot of nerve. By projecting a general image as a faith-healer, he instantly puts himself in a category all by itself. Being different is important if you're planning on succeeding in religion on a grand scale.

Oral Roberts has also said many times, in front of large audiences, that his mother told him, "Oral, be different. Be like Jesus." If you tell that story long enough to enough people, sooner or later some of them will begin to believe that you *are* like Jesus! And that's different, too. Not many human beings are so enamored of themselves that they believe they are like Jesus. Most of us, in possession of our faculties, realize that we're humans and we have no illusions about whether or not we're like Jesus. Further, in realizing that, we wouldn't *begin* to have the nerve to imply that we *might* be like Jesus.

If you want to attract thousands (and then millions) of followers to your ministry, however, some startling innuendo like that is important. It immediately sets you apart from the crowd of the other evangelists who are always present, vying for the attention and money of Christians.

There are other ways of being different. Most ministers tend to use the Bible as a scriptural basis for everything they say. Their sermons tend to be based upon scriptures and are usually couched in scriptural terms. Oral Roberts rather studiously avoids that. He has a way of changing scriptures around and modernizing them so that his sermons sound different than the others we often hear. Most of us have heard sermons that appeal to our inherent sense of guilt about the sins, great or small, that we have committed at some point in our lives: "For we, like sheep, have gone astray." Most preachers, including Billy Graham, appeal to that sense of guilt in order to make us respond in some manner.

Oral Roberts, on the other hand, likes to use scriptures such as John 3:2: "Beloved, I wish above all things that thou mayest prosper and be in good health, even as thy soul prospereth." Oral avoids the guilt syndrome and goes for the desires we all have to succeed, get ahead financially, and live healthy lives. That, in general, makes his ministry different. Also, his sermons, rather than being comprised of scriptural details, will often contain anecdotes and stories about incidents and people that don't have anything to do with the Bible.

His sermons often have stories about one-eyed chickens, holding onto the rope, little boys whipping their little puppies until the puppies' lips begin bleeding, stories about Seed-Faith, falling off bicycles which are demon possessed, or repetitively telling about the death of his oldest daughter. I directed and edited the half-hour television show where Oral and Evelyn sat on a couch and for the first time, told the story of how their daughter, Rebecca, had been killed in a plane crash. It was a heartrending story and their emotions were real. They were actually hurting terribly on that particular morning and all of us had a difficult time working with that telecast. It was an extremely effective show because it was real. It is my contention that Oral later realized just how powerful the show was and he then began telling the story on later telecasts. None of those later programs were as real as the first one, but the story was effective with his audience and it did provide him something different to talk about.

That particular telecast was so powerful and brought such a response in the mail that word got around. Later, Rex Humbard did a similar telecast...and inasmuch as he didn't have a daughter who had died...he used the untimely death of a nephew in copying the success of Oral's program. It was a poor copy of Oral's program and didn't have much impact. It was typical of Rex Humbard, however: sitting there in the number two slot in religious programming, trying to copy Oral in as many ways as possible without being too obvious about it.

One of Oral's closest associates began to worry after Oral had told the story of Rebecca's death several times. The associate's concerns were legitimate because it was beginning to become a little too obvious that Oral was working the incident for everything it was worth. Oral Roberts is a complex human being. I know that he was genuinely shattered by the death of his daughter, Rebecca. I also know that he later used the story to his advantage and told it just a few too many times for it to be a continued valid emotional experience. There were many staff members who felt that even the first program was in poor taste. I disagree and am convinced that first program was legitimate in every way..

Very few of us would be willing to go on national television and bare our pain and our emotions about the death of our daughter. Death, to most of us, is an extremely personal tragedy and we want to be left alone with our loss. Oral Roberts knows this and he relates to personal problems. That is the *only* thing about his entire ministry which I will always believe is valid. He has had problems, he came up from nowhere, and he does personally relate to human suffering. He made the comment on the above telecast that while he had tried in the past to help people who had lost a son or daughter, he didn't really know the pain they were going through until it happened to him. I believe that's true. He also made a comment to the effect that once he *did* realize how much it hurt, he decided to go on television and tell the story and bare his emotions to his followers. In a roundabout way, he was attempting to show that he did understand, that he did know how bad it hurt, that he had felt the pain, and in spite of it all, God was greater than any problem he had...including the terrible loss of his own daughter.

Everyone close to Oral Roberts knows that he always put his ministry before anything else. And he was even willing to reveal his personal agony when it was useful in aiding that ministry. That, in itself, is different.

III. Oral Roberts showing off

The third secret to success in big religion relates to the old adage, "If you want people to think you're getting ahead, you have to *look* like you're getting ahead." Oral Roberts does this with a personal flair that allows him to selectively use other people's ideas to his advantage. He personalizes other people's ideas and alters them to the point that they appear to be original. It is no mere coincidence that the Oral Roberts University campus resembles the buildings usually seen at a world's fair. The architecture reminds you of something very close to Disney World or one of the Six Flags recreational parks. Geodesic domes, parabolic roof structures, round buildings, diamond-shaped buildings, and a prayer tower that is more than vaguely similar to some of the Olympic Towers are part and parcel of the visual impact of Oral Roberts University. On the Oral Roberts University campus, a rectangular building tends to stick out like a sore thumb. It surprises you. Somehow, it just doesn't seem to fit.

It really doesn't look like the typical college campus. In fact, it doesn't look like a college campus at all. But it does hit you right between the eyes. The campus colors are blue and gold. Blue paint and gold-tinted glass. Most of the metal work on the building is gold anodized aluminum. It shows off and it is also *different*.

The basketball team of Oral Roberts University is also meant to show off for Oral Roberts. Most of the players, and there are exceptions, are ones who have athletic ability but have had academic problems getting into other schools. Some of them are players who have been in other schools and dropped out for academic or financial reasons. And, then, some of them are junior college transfers. The junior college transfer game, in basketball, has always amounted to a farm club system for larger colleges who wanted to farm out potentially good players who were perceived to be bad actors or academic risks during the first year or two of college. If the "juco" player succeeds in junior college, makes the adjustment from high school to campus living and develops into a potential blue-chipper, then the major college picks that player up in a hurry.

If a college has enough money, as does Oral Roberts University, it can recruit players heavily, house them in one of the finest athletic dorms in the country, and make up for the fact that the players have to maintain an appearance of being good Christian athletes. The fact that many of them haven't been good Christian athletes is a rather well-hidden secret on the campus. Some of them have been *rumored* to have smoked pot in the athletic dormitory. One of them even got himself shot in a fracas in Las Vegas. Several athletes were involved in an un-Christian involvement with one of the ORU coeds and that, too, was an extremely touchy subject for quite a while.

While those kinds of activities take place on nearly all campuses around the country, one doesn't expect to hear about it on the campus of Oral Roberts University. Regardless, the ORU basketball team has done well over the years and has enjoyed several seasons of 20 wins or more. And when the team gets invited to an NIT Tournament, it is good free publicity for the institution. And that's exactly why the team exists: to win, get invited to tournaments, and to provide publicity for Oral Roberts University.

Oral rationalizes his showing off by saying that when he does something for God, he wants to do it first class. That's a cop-out. Oral is doing it first class because *he* wants it that way.

IV. Oral Roberts changing with the times

Oral has always revealed the capability of keeping ahead of other evangelists. When others were just starting to hold revivals in large churches, he was hitting the road with a tent, the *Canvas Cathedral*, which seated ten thousand. When other evangelists were just beginning to get themselves onto radio stations, Oral was off and running on television. Ask anyone in the know with IBM and you'll hear a story to the effect that the utilization of large computers for mailing lists that go to millions was virtually initiated in Tulsa, Oklahoma, by Oral Roberts.

And while Rex Humbard is preening himself over the completion of his Cathedral of Tomorrow, Oral's basketball team plays in Mabee Center and makes Rex's Cathedral look like a pup tent.

While Reverend Schuler is busy building his church of glass...no one is going to want to throw stones at him...Oral Roberts is off drumming up millions for a City of Faith which includes a 60-story building, a 30-story building, and a 20-story building!

Oral is always one jump ahead...or so it appears. When faith-healing was widely accepted in the fifties, Oral was out there in his tent praying for thousands of hopefuls. When the laying-on-of-the-hands became somewhat suspect, Oral Roberts began talking of healing as something that could affect your finances, your marriage, your job, etc. In short, there are lots of ways that people need a healing. A healing went beyond the physical, it could touch your emotions, your relationships with other people, or your approach to life.

Then, with the announcement of the City of Faith, Oral proposed to combine the power of prayer with the power of medicine into one large medical complex which he maintained would be like nothing in existence. Where does he think all the Presbyterian, Catholic, Baptist, and Methodist hospitals came from? Does he really think he invented holistic medicine? It doesn't matter. There are literally millions who will believe that he did invent holistic medicine and many of them will contribute millions of dollars to help him finance the City of Faith. Those who think that they'll be able to go to the City of Faith for medical care, at little or no cost, will be in for a surprise. When you come to Oral Roberts for anything you bring your pocketbook with you because it's going to cost you a bundle! If you question that, ask the families of the aged who have lived out their last days in Oral Roberts retirement center, University Village. Aged Christians make an outright grant of over $25,000 just to get into Oral's retirement center and they *still* have to pay monthly expenses or sign over major portions of their estate. And when those aged Christians die, the surviving members of the family don't get that initial bequest back. It stays with Oral Roberts...and he stays ahead of the times.

V. Oral Roberts using the media as the message

Before I ever joined the staff of Oral's organization as a television writer, I was asked by his future producer to critique one of Oral's prime-time specials. I was annoyed with the particular special that I was asked to analyze because the director seldom went tighter on Oral than a waist shot. I noticed the expressions on Oral's face and his general countenance. An astute producer/director should have been on a tight shot of Oral's face during his prayer, for example. That tight shot would literally have put Oral's face right into a viewer's living room. His voice and face would be so close to the viewer that, through television, Oral's presence would actually enter the viewer's home.

Oral's future producer agreed with me and later attempted to get Production Associates of Hollywood, Oral's producer at that time, to begin using tighter shots on Oral. Dick Ross apparently didn't agree and in very short order, Oral dropped him as his producer. Oral, himself, recognized the potential power of television as an instrument in big religion. Television, if properly used, can create an atmosphere that is extremely persuasive and utterly convincing. As an example which most of you might remember, it was one thing to read about police dogs being ordered to attack a crowd of black demonstrators. It was quite another thing to actually watch the dogs attack, hear them growl, and hear the screams of pain of the black persons being bitten. When you read of something like that in the paper, it is abstract. You don't really experience the event. However, when you see, hear, and feel it on television, it becomes a real event. You put yourself into the shoes of the person on camera and it is all so visceral or gut-level that you cannot help but become wrapped up in what is happening.

And if you're a television minister who wants to persuade viewers with your sermons and your prayers...and your offers to send a book "at absolutely no obligation on your part"...then the use of that extreme close-up is an awfully effective device. It gets to the point where, just as McLuhan said, the medium *is* the message.

In the Kennedy-Nixon debates, Kennedy looked young and healthy. He was properly dressed for television, had just the right kind and amount of makeup for television, and his hair was done properly. Kennedy was the very picture of health and vitality. Nixon, on the other hand, looked washed out. You could see the top of his head through his thinning hair. What makeup he *did* have on was done improperly and began to run slightly. The overall appearance of Nixon was old, washed out, and slightly evil. And, as we all know, those television debates helped Kennedy win the election.

Oral Roberts also uses professional help to make him look good on television. Two of his former makeup men have also been the makeup artists for "Hotel," "Happy Days," "All in the Family," and "Soap."

The main cameraman who shot all of the aerial photographs for the Alaska show and also shot Oral at the foot of Mt. McKinley in Alaska was John Stevens, one of the cameramen for "Tora, Tora, Tora." The choreographer for Oral's prime-time specials also produces shows in Las Vegas for Andy Williams and the Lennon Sisters.

Oral Roberts wants to look good on television and he's done whatever it took to get him there...using the powerful medium of television to convey his message.

VI. Oral Roberts using transfer of authority

Central, and I mean absolutely central, to the success of Oral's ministry of faith-healing is his use of the transfer of authority. To remind you, Christ was the first human to lay hands upon the sick, heal the blind, and bring the dead back to life. Oral decided to enter the ministry as a faith-healer.

54

Oral Roberts has also said that God told him to take His (God's) healing power to his (Oral's) generation. Further, in one of Oral's recent fund-raising campaigns involving a prayer cloth with Oral's handprint on it, he clearly stated that God had spoken to him 21 times over the years. Oral Roberts is the only evangelist I know of who has kept count of the times God has spoken to him and then revealed that information to his followers. When you tell someone that God has spoken to you, such a statement automatically transfers the authority of God onto you.

How can anyone argue with someone whom God has spoken to? That is, if God really did speak to him. Over the years, I have asked various clergymen if God had ever spoken to them. Almost invariably, they said that while they didn't actually hear God speaking to them, they "felt led" to do things a certain way. On one occasion I asked a pastor that if he "felt led" to persuade his congregation to build a new church, could he then conclude that it had been God who had spoken to him, telling him to have a new church built. The pastor replied, "Well, you *might* say that."

When you are "felt led" to doing something, it could be your subconscious. It could be based upon your opinions. And, if you're inclined to do so, you *could* tell everyone that God had spoken to you.

On one of Oral's telecasts, he stated that God had told him to offer people an opportunity to buy "building blocks" for the City of Faith. Oral also stated that people should buy those "building blocks" for the City of Faith by donating money in multiples of seven. For example: $7.77, $77.77, $777.77, and on up...as long as the donations were in multiples of seven!

What Oral Roberts didn't say was that his father, formerly a minister near Ada, Oklahoma, had built a new church by selling actual concrete blocks to members in the community! One begins to wonder if God spoke to Oral at all about asking people to buy "building blocks." One begins to wonder if, perhaps, Oral remembered that his father had been successful in getting a church built by selling concrete blocks to people in and around Ada, Oklahoma!

Oral Roberts also uses transfer of authority in another, more subtle way...and it involves the latent superstitions we all carry with us, in spite of how much we might deny that we are superstitious. Oral's use of our underlying superstitions is very subtle: he takes advantage of the "good luck" we attribute to the number "seven."

The address of Oral Roberts University is 7777 South Lewis. It could have been any address from 7500 to 8100 on South Lewis because the campus takes up that much space on South Lewis in Tulsa, Oklahoma. However, the number "7777" was chosen.

The telephone number of the prayer tower on the Oral Roberts University campus is 492-7777. It could have been 492-1111 or any other number. However, the one with "7's" was chosen.

When Oral Roberts begins giving sermons to his seminar guests on the ORU campus...the purpose of which is to raise money...one of his sermons will almost invariably contain comments about the powers of the number seven.

Could Oral's use of the number "seven" just be coincidence? Or, could it be that he *knows* people are subconsciously superstitious. And, could it be that he is endeavoring to take advantage of that weakness in all of us?

VII. Instant coffee, instant pudding, instant health, wealth and success...now

We live in an age of more and more things becoming "instant." We buy minute rice, instant tea, instant cocoa, and so on. Ours is a hurry-up society characterized by shortages of time to get everything done which we'd like to accomplish. Instead of spending a Saturday afternoon washing our cars, we drive them through the instant car wash.

Oral Roberts makes use of our inclinations to want things *NOW* by including it in his messages. He says that God is always present at the point of your need and that if you give money away from your need, you can expect back a miracle from God—*Now*. This is a departure from traditional Christian teachings: live the good life, do good deeds, and then someday receive your reward in Heaven.

That's old hat and it won't work on television or through direct mail appeals for money. In order for a television and direct-mail ministry to flourish, it must promise something that isn't being heard anywhere else. Oral knows this and adapts his appeals to fit in with our wishes for things to happen rapidly.

Many of Oral's ending prayers on his television programs go something like this: "...and I pray that as I stretch forth these hands which I've given to God, that a miracle in your finances, in your health, in your marriage, and in your relationships with people will begin to happen *now*, this very day, at this very moment. Amen and Amen."

Then, he'll drop his hands and change his attitude and continue..."and when you write, tell me about your problem. I *love* to hear from you. Your letters mean *so much* to me and Evelyn. And, I'll answer your letter. I answer all my mail and I pray over all your letters. And *now*, as you go through the remainder of this week, remember these words, "Greater is He Who is in you than he who is in the world!" Background music swells up and a catchy tune follows that tends to make you want to tap your foot. When the program ends, it is then time, *now*, to get a pencil and paper and write to Oral Roberts, ask for his latest book, and include a check which isn't post-dated. Date it today...in the *now*!

Chapter 4

Oral's Kingdom for a Slogan: "Something Good is Going to Happen to You"

Something Good is Going to Happen to You

Most successful evangelists today have some sort of slogan that appeals to people's desires to get *ahead* in life. It's the new Christianity...God wants you to have lots of money and be happy! The old, out-moded doctrines of living the good life, doing good deeds, and getting your reward in heaven have been replaced by modern-day evangelical variations of Positive Thinking.

Reverend Schuler has coined the terminology, "Possibility Thinking" and the core of that philosophy is that you can do anything you want to do (including financially). Implicit in this is that it helps if you listen to him, subscribe to his programs, send in for his books...and contribute to his ministry.

Oral Roberts, however, is credited with starting the whole thing. In the earlier years of his ministry, he used to tell his audience that his mother had told him, "Oral, be different from other men. Be like Jesus." In saying that to people, of course, the implied message was that he *was* and *is* like Jesus. A certain amount of authority was conferred upon him by his admirers and Oral did, indeed, attempt to be like Jesus in praying for the sick. In seeking ways to make his ministry succeed, Oral needed to place himself on a plateau that wasn't occupied by the other evangelists and faith-healers who were getting started about the same time he was.

And then Oral hit upon something that was more powerful than anything he had ever tried before. He broke away from traditional Christian messages and tested the Positive Thinking waters...by appealing to people's universal desires to improve their situation in life. And, boy, did he hit it right!

"Something Good is Going to Happen to You." The first time I heard that, in the mid-sixties, it impressed me. That was one *extremely* effective slogan. I realized it had a potent message for most Christians: they could live the good life, love Jesus and still be able to become wealthy without having their consciences bother them. One of Oral's associates sent me a little desk placard that had the above saying on it and I placed it on my credenza behind my desk while I was on the staff of another university. When I'd interview prospective secretaries for jobs within my office, they'd see and read the sign. Some of them would smile a little, others would almost completely lose their train of thought as I asked them questions about their experience and training, and some of them would really respond to the little sign and do their absolute best to impress me. They wanted a job in an office that openly stated "something good was going to happen to them." Since Oral's television program wasn't being aired in the area at that time, none of them appeared to know the origins of the little placard, and they'd react in ways that had nothing to do with religion. Alumni who happened to walk into my office would read the placard and ask, "Where'd you get that? I'd like to have one for my office!"

The slogan worked! It aroused people's interest and made them think. I am absolutely certain that some of them thought about it enough that they stopped by my office after having visited the campus to write out a check to the university! After all, "something good was going to happen to them." The little slogan on the placard made people feel good.

In other words, the slogan appealed to people simply because of its intrinsic effect. People who didn't even know the slogan's origin responded to that message...because they *wanted* to believe it. *Everyone* wants something good to happen to them. Everyone wants to win the Sweepstakes Prize; everyone wants to win lots of money on the TV game show; everyone wants some obscure relative to leave them millions of dollars...everyone wants to get ahead financially in life and have as few problems as possible. The slogan doesn't necessarily have anything to do with religion. Instead, it pulls at, and appeals to, basic human psychological motivations.

And all ministers appeal to what are basically psychological weaknesses in all of us. Religion scares most people. People become Christians because they don't want to go to Hell when they die. They pray before going to bed that they won't die in their sleep...but just in case they do, they pray and confess their sins of the day, ask forgiveness and then go off to sleep, safe in the knowledge that if they do "pass away" in the middle of the night, everything will be all right and they'll wake up in Heaven.

Religion also appeals to our inherent sense of guilt. All of us do things occasionally which we know aren't proper. It's a basic human weakness to fail once in a while and do something we wish we hadn't done. And, that sense of guilt is something that evangelists use to their benefit.

Oral Roberts once said, "In nearly all cases, a sense of guilt precedes a religious experience." What he was saying was that it takes a feeling of guilt, followed by a desire to "make it right," to cause people to get out of their chairs and come down to the altar. Billy Graham's Crusades are the best example of this: he preaches Hellfire and Brimstone, makes his audiences feel guilty about their sins, and then gives an "altar call" which is accompanied by religious music which pulls at the emotions and the heartstrings. During one of Billy's Crusades, literally hundreds of people will leave their chairs and walk down to the altar to receive prayers of forgiveness. These prayers of forgiveness lead the person who has sinned through an emotional catharsis so he feels that he is cleansed of his sins and can then "start the next day right." That sort of experience generally makes people feel good. Most of us have been through it at some point in our lives in one way or another. In another way, as children we have often felt better after a good spanking and a scolding, followed by loving hugs, than we did moments before the spanking. The experience of being spanked, scolded, and then loved left us feeling like we were now "good little boys and girls." And BIG EVANGELISTS, in BIG RELIGION, work on that same basic principle.

Oral Roberts, however, found a way to do it without having to prey on that innate sense of guilt we all carry with us. His slogan took you, the viewer or the reader, from whatever plateau you happened to be on, and carried you immediately into the psychological realm of "something good happening to you." He didn't have to waste time, money, or words building you up, conditioning you, and getting you ready for an "altar call." His new way allowed him to take you, the sinner, into the world of "good things" *right away*, in the NOW.

"IN THE NOW" is an important element of Oral's messages. He doesn't talk about living a restrained life filled with good deeds that will ultimately put you into Heaven. He says that "something good is going to happen to you" *NOW!* That appeals to people. Folks don't like to wait until they go to Heaven for something good to happen to them. They want it to happen NOW! And so, Oral says that it *can* happen NOW. You don't have to wait to go to Heaven; you don't have to lead a life that is filled with restraints; you don't have to worry constantly about your sins and you don't have to feel that being a Christian necessarily puts you into a category of being a second-class citizen.

All of these slogans have extremely popular appeal. Such slogans promise improvements in our lives *right away* from a God who is good and looks down upon us, not in wrath over our sins, but with loving, understanding beneficence. He understands all our human frailties and loves us anyway, and is going to heap all sorts of good things on us *no matter what!*

This approach is *the one thing* that put Oral in a different camp than most ministers or evangelists. While most ministers in local churches are either preaching or talking about sins, the repenting of sins in order to enter Heaven, or trying to get people to tithe (giving 10% of their income to the Church), Oral Roberts is showing increasing numbers of people an easier way to do it.

The Evangelical, Charismatic approach to Christianity... combined with a concept called Seed-Faith...is what put Oral Roberts into a different league than all other television ministries. It's also what put the rest of them scurrying wildly about in search of ways to copy his formula without being too obvious about it.

The Reverend Schuler's concept of "Possibility Thinking" is nothing more than a variation of Oral's theme, Seed-Faith. Schuler's "Possibility Thinking" is very simply paraphrased into "you are what you want to be."

Reverend Ike's formula, also a seeming copy of Oral's methods, is an extremely blatant example of a money approach to Chistianity. Reverend Ike openly flaunts money, the desire for money, the need for money, and the love of money as a method of improving your life...and he somehow manages to combine *that* with Christianity. The money-changers whom Christ drove out of the temple would absolutely salivate rivers if they could have a chance to get in on the kind of action that the Reverend Ike indulges himself in when it comes to passing the offering plate.

None of them, however, have enjoyed the financial success that Oral Roberts likes to play down. While he has built a $50 million campus with contributed funds, mounted a basketball team continually kept in the public's eyes through winning and being invited to NIT and NCAA tournaments, begun a law school, dental school, medical school, and supported a television ministry that is the *largest syndicated television show in the world,* Oral Roberts still isn't satisfied. He wants to build a City of Faith, the construction of which will set the medical community back on its ears and, ultimately, set the public back onto its checkbook because of the impact it will have on health care costs in Tulsa and the state of Oklahoma. But, Oral doesn't really care about the impact his proposed City of Faith will have in "his" community. He is looking forward to his last years and wants to go out with his entire life and ministry legitimized through the completion of a medical complex that combines prayer with medicine.

It's almost as if Oral Roberts has finally matured in his approach to religion and medicine. He surely knows the skepticism about anyone ever being healed in any of his campaigns. (I never saw it happen.) Now as an adjunct to his "university," he wants to build a complex that will "prove" that prayer and medicine *do* go hand in hand...as long as it's done his way.

The fact that the holistic approach to medicine has been practiced by the Catholic Church for centuries does not deter Oral Roberts from implying that his City of Faith will be a revolutionary approach to the delivery of health care in Tulsa, Oklahoma, and the United States.

He started out in 1977 by announcing the City of Faith, indicating that it would be built through "miracles from Heaven in '77!" Further, he went on in 1978 by promising that "God won't be late in '78."

When he appeared on the Tomorrow Show with Tom Snyder, on Feb. 19, 1979, Oral ended the program with another slogan, "Miracles will be *mine* in '79!"

Slogans are often a dime a dozen. Oral exhibits the capability to take a ten-cent slogan and turn it into millions of dollars. While he has unabashedly admitted that the cost of the City of Faith may approach $100 million, other informed medical personnel tend to believe that the actual costs of completing a 777 bed hospital, research center, and clinic will go as high as $400 million. The average state (and you can pick any one of them out of the current 50) would have great reservations about attempting to fund such a project. But, Oral's ministry goes beyond the budget of what a state often spends. Oral says he'll build the City of Faith and complete it debt-free!

Experts in the field of health care indicate that the operating budget of the City of Faith *alone* will run in the vicinity of $75 million. Where is that money going to come from? The federal government? Through Medicare and Medicaid payments? From NIH grants? There simply is *no way* that Oral Roberts can repeatedly raise that kind of money himself. And when *he* dies, many ORU staffers feel there is no way that Richard Roberts (Oral's son) will be capable of carrying on the thrust of Oral's ministry.

Perhaps the City of Tulsa will acquire a Prayer Tower and the City of Faith by default on unpaid water and gas bills!

The Prayer Tower could be turned into a small, avante garde restaurant with cuisine described as "simply heavenly!"

The City of Faith could be turned into a hotel complex to house viewers who come from miles around to participate in the Great River Raft Race that takes place in Tulsa each year.

In any case, the City of Tulsa shouldn't count on any of the facilities at ORU lasting very long. One ORU vice-president made the comment, "We only build a building to last twenty-five years, anyway!" Now, does that tell you anything?

One of Oral Robert's slogans that has helped him in his fund-raising efforts over the years relates to his use of the terminology, "Point of Contact." Oral Roberts used the "point of contact" to persuade his radio and television audience to lay their hands upon their home set and allow *that* to be the point of contact between Oral and the person who needed a healing.

In some of those broadcasts, Oral would state that he felt a warmth in his hand and said that the warmth indicated God's presence. Supposedly, as Oral prayed on the radio, holding his mike in his hand, the healing powers of God would travel through the radio waves and be there for anyone's use who merely reached out and touched their radios!

When Oral discussed the possibility of using the principle on television, he talked with aides about actually laying his hand on the front of a television camera...or, because of technical limitations of television cameras, laying his hand upon a pane of glass in front of the television camera. The shot would look, on the home sets, as if Oral's hand was actually pressed up against the inside of the viewer's home television set! Oral would then have his television audience put their own hand up against Oral's on their home sets! One aide who heard the story through the organizational grapevine thought the idea was preposterous and made the mistake of telling Oral that he thought it was the "stupidest" idea he had ever heard of. He didn't know the idea was Oral's. In short order, Oral let the man know that the idea was *his* and that it *was not* a stupid idea at all!

The man then informed me, after that blunder, he didn't get a raise for over five years! *"A man who does not know forgiveness in his own heart cannot know God."*

As this book is being written, it is being rumored in Tulsa that Oral Roberts is having problems raising money for the City of Faith. On the construction site, it sometimes appears as if there is very little real activity going on. Perhaps there is some truth to the rumors that Oral's seemingly bottomless coffers are, indeed, running dry. If that's the case, Oral will probably come up with another slogan to help him out of his dilemma: *"Help me on payday in nineteen-eighty!"* Or, inasmuch as contributions to the City of Faith are tax-deductible, he might coin the phrase, "The City of Faith will touch the skies. Send donations and itemize!"

Whatever phrase Oral Roberts decides to use to help him complete the City of Faith, you can bet your last dollar on one thing: it will have *something* to do with money, *somehow!*

Chapter 5

Oral Roberts University, The Faculty, The World Action Singers and Other Student Activities

The campus

As stated elsewhere, the campus of Oral Roberts University is referred to by many students as "Six Flags over Jesus." The main entrance to the campus contains an avenue of flags which purports to represent the countries of the students who attend the institution. The general visual impact of the campus is not at all unlike the effect of one of America's recreational parks...such as one of the Six Flags facilities. Smacking the campus visitor right in the eye are the blue and gold colors which cover nearly every building. Blue paint and gold anodized aluminum...or gold colored glass. The general appearance is *very* modern.

It has a rather soothing effect on the average visitor and that could be attributed primarily to the color scheme and the sloping hills on which the campus is located. If you drove by the campus and had absolutely no idea that it was Oral Roberts University, you would still probably conclude that it was some kind of religious institution. The prayer tower, of course, pointing up into the sky, would tend to lead a viewer to that assumption; but the simple beauty of the chapel is really the visual highlight of the campus. While some of the other buildings on the campus appear to be somewhat "forced," the chapel is at peace with its shape and its location near the front of the campus.

In general, all college campuses tend to have something about them which is either unique or serves to affect the general atmosphere which prevails throughout the faculty and student body. Inasmuch as the prayer tower is in the center of the campus at ORU and no student or faculty member can cross the campus without going relatively near the prayer tower, one could surmise that the structure's general effect is one which conveys and rather subtly dictates a general aura of quiet peaceful spiritualism.

The architectural statement which the campus makes would lead a visitor to think that Oral Roberts University was a peaceful, harmonious place to pursue an education. That *could* be true...if the president, the administration, and the majority of the faculty were to somehow be removed and replaced by other professional educators from within the academic community in the United States! And while that statement may appear to be rather broad-sweeping, harsh, or even unfair, it does reflect the opinions of many who have worked at Oral Roberts University and subsequently left for justifiable reasons. I have heard many people who came to Oral Roberts University...as a result of the smooth recruiting "treatment" which prospective staff members get...later comment that they had never worked on a campus which was so "un-Christian." I've heard many relative newcomers make comments to the effect that the campus they left was more Christian and had more good people working for it than Oral Roberts University did. And after you've been there a while yourself, you come to understand what they meant.

Faculty and administrative types at Oral Roberts University

The president of the average accredited university generally has *some* kind of degree. Most often, a university president has an earned doctorate. Oral Roberts does not have an earned

67

doctorate. In fact, he doesn't have an earned degree of *any* kind.

There are other persons on the staff at Oral Roberts University who do not hold degrees of any kind...and, again, I'm speaking of *earned* degrees. An honorary degree, from an academic perspective, isn't worth the paper it's written on. Most academic institutions have either a faculty handbook or a university catalog which lists its faculty and staff along with their academic backgrounds. For example: John Doe; B. S., MSU: M.S., MIT: Ph.D., Harvard. Such publications will often also include the dates on which such faculty and staff received their degrees.

The Faculty Handbook at Oral Roberts University has faculty members who show such listings. There are, however, certain vagaries used in the Handbook which reveal that certain administrators don't have any degrees at all...just like Oral. When a person hasn't received the expected bonafide degree, whether undergraduate or graduate, the wording used is like this: "completed his studies at MTU," *or* "pursued his studies at MBU." You get the point: the listing merely states that the indicated faculty or other staff member completed studies there—the individual finished his studies but didn't fulfill the requirements for the particular undergraduate or graduate degree. Whatever the listing suggests, the fact is that the person didn't get the degree. What academic institution of reputation that you know practices this kind of vagary when listing credentials?

The Dean of Women at Oral Roberts University has no degree. Most Deans of Women do have degrees of *some* kind. The vice-president for Student Affairs "completed his studies at Tulsa University."

The man formerly filling the position of Chief of Staff at Oral Roberts University, which would presumably include the medical school and the City of Faith, had a degree that he'd received from Southern California Bible College, an institution that was not accredited at the time he received it. Upon graduation from SCBC, he taught for a portion of one academic year at an Iowa high school. When school officials learned he didn't have an accredited degree, he was not allowed to continue teaching. Then he became Chief of Staff of Oral Roberts University! Once, when asked where he went to college, he replied, "Southern Cal." *Southern Cal, indeed.* Southern California Bible College! The man graduated in the fifties. The school finally became accredited in the mid-sixties.

There is nothing intrinsically snobbish about holding a college degree. There are all types of degrees. A licensed electrician has a "degree"...that license tells people that the electrician knows what he's doing. Similarly, when an institution of higher learning, such as a college or university, is offering bachelor's degrees to undergraduate students, the general practice is that all faculty and staff need degrees in order to be capable of teaching in or managing such an institution. When an institution seeks to hide the fact that some of its top people either don't have accredited degrees or any degrees at all, then most academicians would concur something was wrong. But then, when the president of the institution himself doesn't have a degree, what difference does it make if some of his top people don't have one either?

People generally go to work for Oral Roberts University for a reason. More specifically, they left something else behind (which didn't satisfy them), and gravitated to Oral Roberts University because of some kind of need in either their personal or professional life...usually their personal life. Sort of like, "Well, I've tried everything else. Perhaps this will work out." It is also interesting to note that nearly all the men and women who work for the man, Oral Roberts, fit rather neatly into one of five categories.

The first and most obvious category is the dedicated, true-blue Christian...and there are a few of those still around. Such people go to work for Oral Roberts University because they can't tolerate working in the real-world environment where they have to associate with ordinary sinners who swear occasionally, sip a beer or two, or errantly smoke cigarettes in public. There are Christian types who simply don't want to be around anyone else who isn't also a Christian. I call it the "convent complex": taking its shape in the form of Christians who simply want to isolate themselves among other Christians. This is a very sterile form of Christianity.

The smell of sin appears to send shudders of revulsion up and down their charismatic spines and, upon reading or hearing about some sinful activity, you'll occasionally observe them huddled together in armwaving, lip-trembling prayer groups, pleading for the second coming of Christ! If Jesus Christ, Himself, had done that, we never would have heard about Him today...and there would be no such thing as modern Christianity.

The second major category of employee to be found on the Oral Roberts University campus is the closet sinner. Some would call these types hypocrites. Regardless of what you choose to call them, they put on the appearance of being Christians, but in very sneaky ways they sin as much or more than the average man on the street. Oh, they go to church and have even been observed to speak in tongues, *but boy can they sin!* And before making any further comments, I should reveal that *my* church allows me to drink socially and does not frown upon the use of tobacco, except as a possible health hazard. In other words, if I'm going to be considered a sinner by some, then I'm going to have to be considered as being open about it, rather than being a closet sinner.

But what about the "Christian" who would swear on a stack of Bibles that he doesn't smoke or drink, or even swear but does, in fact, do all those things in private? Two of Oral Roberts' vice-presidents smoke and drink...generally when they're out of town on business. I was on a plane with one of them and the man got so drunk that a friend and I had to help carry him off the plane. Now, I don't mind admitting to you that I was embarrassed by that incident. I never experienced anything like that on the other two campuses for which I worked and it seemed exceptionally inappropriate as an employee of Oral Roberts University.

Later, on that same business trip, the same man and I went into a place in Hollywood called "Whiskey 'a Go Go" and listened to music and had a few cocktails. In my book, the activity was considered acceptable. The gentleman, however, made a point of asking me not to mention *anything* about the plane trip *or* the evening spent in "Whiskey 'a Go Go."

The high school daughter of this same man once drove up to their house with a school friend and sat outside in the driveway smoking a cigarette. The man came out and told his daughter that if she was going to smoke, could she please do it in the backyard on the patio rather than out on the driveway where other ORU employees, or even Oral Roberts, might see her smoking. He didn't ask his daughter not to smoke. He merely asked her not to smoke where she might be seen. Some would call that discretion; others would call it hypocrisy. Some would call it fear.

On several occasions when I was on the West Coast with one ORU vice-president and another employee who was referred to as Richard's babysitter, we stayed at the Holiday Inn in Hollywood. Often, at the end of a day of editing half-hour shows for Oral Roberts at Vidtronics, we would walk into the lounge and have a couple of drinks. It was a quiet, respectable lounge filled with other businessmen who were temporarily in Hollywood. One time, however, as we were seated in the lounge with drinks, a man walked by outside who made both of the above gentlemen very nervous. He was an ORU graduate by the name of Tom Ivy who, at that time, was the director for Billy Graham's television crusades. Neither of the men with me wanted him to see them in that lounge. I was aware that Tom Ivy knew several people back on the ORU campus and that is perhaps why they became so nervous. They didn't want him telling anyone back in Tulsa that an ORU vice-president and Richard's assistant were seen drinking in a Hollywood lounge. Discretion or hypocrisy?

There are other types of closet sinners at Oral Roberts University: the charismatic homosexuals who perhaps go to ORU in search of a halfway house, porno buffs who would absolutely die of apoplexy if they were named, die-hard adulterers who make trips out-of-town for group sex, and finally, step-and-fetch-it cussers...people on campus who really love to swear so much that they take the time to invent new and acceptable ways of using expletives. I must admit that I rather admired the ingenuity of some of these inventions: "I don't give a rip" or "Go pray for yourself" in place of other expressions using four letter words.

The point is very simply this: the institution, Oral Roberts University, likes to present itself as *the* holy school in the world, *and it isn't!* And it isn't that what some employees do is all that wrong. But, when they do things they don't wish anyone to know about, then *they* must consider it wrong and they should probably stop doing those things they worry so much about. To put it very clearly, Oral Roberts University has the same kind of people on its campus that are found to be walking down any back street in any town in California. But, you'd never get anyone there to admit it publicly. Not on your life!

The third major category of faculty member to be found at Oral Roberts University is the losers. They're the bottom half of the M.S. and Ph.D. barrel who simply don't have much luck finding academic jobs at other institutions with higher standards. If they could, they would, but they can't, so they don't. These are the people who somehow managed to squeak through an academic program which awarded them a piece of paper labelling them forever after as mediocre. Nearly every graduate school has *some* kind of program which does this kind of thing: and it's usually found somewhere within colleges of education. I am not going to even bother to substantiate this comment or attempt to prove that this category of academician exists. Simply ask any faculty member of an institution with even a good academic reputation and he'll nod his head in the affirmative...as long as you don't attempt to get him to admit that any of *his* graduate students got through on such a program! These losers are the people you feel sorry for: they are allowed to muddle their way through a graduate program and receive a Ph.D...and they nearly always end up teaching in some school like Oral Roberts University.

The fourth category of person to be found working at Oral Roberts University is often the most interesting: the kind who wants to somehow become another Oral Roberts. They're the people with enormous egos, or the students who firmly believe they'll graduate with a Bachelor's in Theology and go out there and immediately step into their own "worldwide ministry." They're also the World Action Singers who hope they'll be discovered by Hollywood because of singing on Oral's television shows. And then there are the pathetic scores of students and staff who have higher expectations than abilities. They desperately want to be someone, but they don't know how to go about it. They cling to the phrase, "Something Good is Going to Happen to You," smiling benignly, muttering in tongues, awaiting that cataclysmic bolt of lightning that will turn them into "somebody." There seems to be something about Oral Roberts that attracts the unfulfilled person. And there is nothing intrinsically wrong with that... Christ attracted thousands of unfulfilled people. But, *He* delivered on a direct, personal level. Oral Roberts *does not!* When the show is over, the TV camera turned off, when the last buck has been brought in from a fund-raising seminar, Oral won't be found in the presence of anyone with needs. He'll be found on the golf course at Southern Hills Country Club, getting over having rubbed shoulders with the masses. That sounds incongruous, but from working with him, I've found that Oral dislikes being around anyone lower than himself.

And he hates being around a sick person. He is repulsed by sickness or poverty, and he can go into a rage at the thought of someone wanting to get their ministry started from his campus. He made a statement in Chapel once that if anyone on campus wanted to get their "own ministry" going, they could. Just don't expect to get it started here on *this* campus. You can go out and do it on your own!

The fifth and final type of person to be found on the campus of Oral Roberts University has already been lightly touched upon in previous paragraphs...in that this type has some of the characteristics of the unfulfilled who want to become another Oral Roberts or someone like him. They're the men and women with human needs in their lives, the people who have had something cut them down, who have been hurt by life, or been deflated by the recognition of their own inadequacies in dealing with life and its problems. Most of them are real people whom you, the reader, would probably like. They are ordinary people, looking for a better shot, another chance, searching for a way to solve the problem that brought them to ORU in the first place. It is these people, I perceive, who make up the bulk of the personnel force of Oral Roberts University: the ones who have certain abilities to get jobs done, who work for a cause that makes them feel better about themselves and life, and get some of their own needs met through the work they do for Oral Roberts. These people are the only *real* aspect of the whole shootin' match at ORU. And, they're the ones Oral Roberts takes advantage of.

The curriculum at
Oral Roberts University

The general opinion of the curricular offerings at Oral Roberts University seems to be favorable, even complimentary. One vice-president admits, however, that the institution is overrated academically. While the dial-access information retrieval system on display in the Learning Resources Center is rather impressive, one often finds students sitting in the learning carrels, watching cartoons with their headsets on. Nearly all of the classrooms in the Learning Resources Center (the LRC) have television monitors which are tied into a video-distribution center which can play several programs simultaneously to different classes being held in the LRC. The system would appear to epitomize the use of audio/visual techniques to enhance the learning process with students at ORU.

The Vice-President for Academic Affairs has confided, however, that the real purpose of the system was meant to keep instructional costs per student down. The system reportedly was installed with the aid of a Title I Grant from the federal government under the Higher Education Act. The amount of the grant was $520,000 and served to defray costs of installing the video-distribution system in the LRC. At first blush, and with a minimum of exposure to the system, the casual observer would conclude that the system provided a wide array of educational materials available for instant call-up and display to student groups. On the surface that is true. But, the real problem relating to effective use of a video-distribution system lies in the quality of the programs being aired.

For years, the quality of the programming used on the system was extremely low. Most of the video packages consisted of nothing more than slide shows recorded on video cassettes for distribution purposes through the system. As a writer myself, I was appalled at the quality of the materials used, the rather sloppy manner in which the packages were written, and the poor camera techniques used in recording the slides themselves. Most of the camera shots were static. There were no zooms, no pans, no tilts, no racks, and no dissolves. The rather large assemblage of video cassettes used to instruct students consisted of little more than one camera cut after another of boring slides. Quite often, students would sit in class listening to a five-minute narrative comment as they watched *one* slide.

Any specialist in Instructional Design will immediately agree that the biggest problem involved in putting together a quality learning instrument lies in the preparation and acquisition stages. Input from interested and dedicated faculty is a *must*. If the Instructional Designer cannot get the cooperation of a faculty member who, by necessity, must function as a "content specialist" in the academic discipline being treated, the final product will ultimately turn out to be something less than optimum. It may even contain gross inaccuracies. In several instances, I found that Media Specialists...people who are trained to use various media in an educational manner...were actually writing the scripts and shooting the slides to be put together into an educational package. A Media Specialist is definitely *not* an Instructional Designer. An Instructional Designer often has at least a Master's degree in education and will often tend to specialize in a certain discipline or group of related disciplines. A Media Specialist, on the other hand, often has only a Bachelor's degree...and while that may qualify him to work with media as a learning tool, it *absolutely does not* qualify him to select instructional materials, make qualitative judgments about content, or write an instructional script without benefit of academic input.

For years at Oral Roberts University, that was the way it was done. One "Media Specialist" did not even have his Bachelor's degree in that field! In other words, a person without even an undergraduate degree was actually writing instructional scripts, choosing which slides would be videotaped, and editing the materials together himself. The irony of the whole thing was that of all the Media Specialists, he *did* have the most talent! Still, that doesn't justify using him in a capacity where so much error could be introduced into the instructional process.

Because of space and time problems in the LRC, the educational media people began using some of the television production facilities in the building which I managed...Oral Roberts Television Productions. My operation, at that time, had nothing to do with the production of instructional materials. Its responsibilities were confined to the production of ministry productions, specials, sports events, and other occasional productions such as Miss Teenage America, Positive Thinking Rallies, etc. In other words, my department handled everything but instructional productions. As the Educational Media personnel began using our facilities, it became apparent to my staff and me that the materials being put together by Ed Media were not the caliber of productions we were accustomed to working with.

I discussed the matter with an ORU vice-president eventually, and began to relate what I considered to be potential and present problems with the manner in which instructional materials were being produced. To my chagrin, it wasn't long before *I* was given that production responsibility along with my other duties.

Immediately I requested an operational and functional separation between the duties of an Instructional Designer and a Media Specialist. The Vice-President for Learning Resources began to give me "practical" reasons why some of the Media Specialists would continue to have to totally prepare instructional scripts and video-learning packages. I dug my heels in and refused to agree and eventually the University hired two more Instructional Designers to interface with the faculty, produce course syllabi, and proceed with the preparation of an instructional script. Once that was done, the final script would be given to a Media Specialist and that person would shoot the script on videotape and ready it for distribution through the system.

I also established a committee to critique the "final" productions and provide for final approval or recommendations for changes in video packages *before* they went onto the system. Prior to that, no such committee had even existed. Often, no one had seen some of the video packages...other than the Vice-President for Learning Resources...until they were aired on the system. And that included the faculty members who were *supposed* to be providing substantive input into the production of those materials! When I left Oral Roberts University, there were four Media Specialists working in Educational Television Productions (which I'd formed) and three Instructional Designers working in the Department of Instructional Design...which I had suggested be formed.

In any event, once a clear-cut separation of duties and qualifications was made, the quality of the learning instruments being recorded on videotape went up markedly. Students began making comments about how much they appreciated and enjoyed, *and learned from,* the new video productions we had made. Faculty members became interested and inquired about getting involved. And while the Vice-President for Learning Resources won't like to hear about it, I maintain that things would still be going on in the same old shabby manner if something hadn't been done. The point is, that from 1965 through 1976, many of the productions being aired on the video-distribution system were being produced by unqualified personnel! And when a video-distribution system is as critical to the instructional process as it is at ORU, you can make your own conclusions about the relative quality of the education that many ORU students were getting in core courses.

Having worked on two other large and reputable campuses, I was naturally interested in the quality of the curricula on the ORU campus. In some instances, I was very impressed, and in others I was rather disappointed. From my observations, the following degree programs at ORU would rate on a par with some of the best available: Nursing, Television Productions, Music, and also the M.B.A. program. Other degree tracks, which haven't been in existence long enough to prove whether or not they'll cut the mustard, may make the grade eventually.

From all appearances, I suspect that the professional programs in Law and Dentistry are "sleepers." In other words, they may become better programs than one might expect.

Whatever you do, don't send your offspring to ORU to get one of those obscure degrees in Interpersonal Communications. And don't let them major in English at ORU either. I saw several seniors in English diagramming sentences. When you're a college senior in an English department, you shouldn't still be diagramming sentences! Something's wrong there.

Dress code and conduct

ORU is the only "university" campus I know of that requires its male students to wear ties to class. I've seen several male students dressed in levis and loafers, with sport shirts on, hurrying out of their dorms putting ties around their necks. Women must wear skirts and blouses to class. They cannot wear slacks or shorts, or sandals, or that sort of thing. One ORU vice-president stated that Oral viewed the ORU dress code as the last hold-out which kept his campus from becoming like all the others. Oral Roberts sees the acquiescence to the dress code as an acceptance of the institution's authority over its students. As long as students are required to wear ties and skirts, they won't be getting involved in demonstrations or other types of peaceful dissent. Being familiar with Oral's rather authoritarian approach to running a campus, I rather doubt that he'd consider *any* type of dissent to be "peaceful."

Theoretically, no sinful conduct takes place on the ORU campus. "Students don't smoke, and they don't chew, and they don't truck with those who do!" *Baloney!* I've known ORU students (who are now on the ORU staff) who had refrigerators hidden in the dormitories which they kept filled with beer. If all the male students had absolutely no inclination to hit some of the bars in north Tulsa on Friday night, the Dean of Students wouldn't have any reason to be making the rounds checking up on whether some of "his men" might be tippling just a bit. The Dean of Men reportedly issued an edict that no male students would give each other backrubs. Such activity could lead to homosexuality!

Sex at ORU?

One wonders if perhaps any of those Christian students at ORU ever indulge in the rigors of human passion. College students have been known to do those sorts of things...and, from the stories, it would appear that ORU is really no different than other campuses when it comes to sex. There might be one exception: many of the students at ORU tend to date students of the opposite sex at Tulsa University. In the past, a few ORU students who "went all the way" and later got "convicted" about their transgressions confessed their sins during devotions or to counselors in Student Affairs. That sort of confession at ORU can get you kicked out of school! Therefore, students who *might* be inclined to make a "mistake" tend to date Tulsa University students. The word is, students at Tulsa University don't kiss and tell!

One particularly humorous story that was told by a Tulsa University student follows: he was dating an ORU coed and one evening they got to breathing heavily and the young lady exclaimed, "Oh, I *know* this isn't the Lord's will, but it feels so good I can't stop!"

One of the married faculty members who teaches a course on marriage and family told the class that sometimes, during the frenzied ecstasy of orgasm, he broke into the language of the spirit. For those of you who don't understand what that means, he was saying that he spoke in tongues when he climaxed. By Golly, I've felt that good a few times myself, and while I don't do what he did, I'm not going to criticize that faculty member at all! If his religion serves him *that* well, more power to him! Just remember, I'm talking about *marital* bliss!

The World Action Singers

Many other students on the ORU campus call the World Action Singers the Worldly Action *Swingers*. During my years at ORU, I heard a lot of stories about escapades involving the World Action Singers who appear on television with Oral Roberts. They also back up Richard when he sings on TV and some of them accompany him when he goes on the road for his "Partners Meetings." While I won't tell any stories about the Singers that I heard from other people, I do feel justified in telling what I personally observed. Most of the World Action Singers have truly been outstanding young Christian men and women. Inasmuch as I had to work rather closely with them during several television productions, I came to feel almost like a father to some of them. However, a few did have a bit of the "devil" in them. And, again, I want to state that what may be acceptable at other places is not often acceptable at ORU. And if it isn't acceptable, it shouldn't go on. Right? So, all I'm revealing is what shouldn't go on!

When we videotaped the Alaska special, the entire production crew *and the cast* had a free evening in Juneau, Alaska. Some of us ended up at a night club named "Annabelle Lee's." It was on the waterfront, had a good view of the bay, revealed a good menu, and sported a live band that wasn't too bad...but not as good musically as some of the World Action Singers. In a short time, some of the Singers took over for the band, picked up their instruments and began singing some of those "worldly" songs. The Singers were better than the band that had been paid to perform! I began dancing with a young lady who was an assistant out of the Alaska Lieutenant Governor's office and as I whirled around the floor, I saw one older, longtime employee of Oral's really "cuttin' the rug" with a woman who ran the gift shop in the Baranof Hotel...where we were staying while in Juneau. I danced up near the band and got the attention of a Singer who, at that time, was singing lead vocal. I pointed toward the old-time employee of Oral's who was on the floor cutting up, and when the young man saw what I was pointing at, he couldn't sing anymore. He began laughing, busted the number up, and the rest of the band started laughing also. The old-timer became mildly annoyed and instructed the band to keep on playing. They did and we resumed dancing. It was *good, clean fun* and we all enjoyed it.

Later, some of the Singers went back to their tables and ordered drinks with their meals. Unfortunately for them, a staff member walked in who was supposed to be in charge of the Singers and he instructed them to either get rid of their drinks *or* leave the premises. He commented that it wouldn't do for anyone associated with Oral Roberts to be seen drinking in a night club.

Some of them did get up and leave. Later in the evening, on the way back to the hotel, I stopped in to take a look at a famous tavern in Juneau...the Red Dog Saloon. I noticed some of the Singers inside, quietly enjoying themselves so I went on toward the hotel and didn't say anything. I later got chewed out a little for not running everyone out of *both* places. I replied that if half the production crew was there, what difference did it make if some of the cast were also enjoying themselves. The individual who was attempting to scold me replied, "Never mind." The night before that, he had me take a six-pack of beer to *his* room for *him*. Certainly in this instance he was one of the closet sinners.

My biggest problem with the World Action Singers stemmed from our location taping on Grandfather Mountain in North Carolina. The owner of Grandfather Mountain was gracious enough to allow the World Action Singers to stay in condominiums which were part of the Grandfather Mountain Country Club complex. The Singers partied quite a bit and broke up some of the furniture in the condominiums. One of my staff members who was an ORU graduate himself showed me a Polaroid picture of some Singers with beer cans in one hand and cigarettes in the other. Annoyed with him, I asked him to destroy the pictures. I'd gotten the message by then and I knew that if one of those pictures got into the papers, the faces would be familiar to many of Oral Roberts' followers. Later, I told the producer about the incident and he became very upset that pictures had been taken. He didn't quiet down until I assured him that the pictures had been destroyed.

The actual owner of one of the condominiums called me later...after we had arrived back in Tulsa...and complained about the damage that had been done to his property. Cigarette burns had been made on dinette and coffee tables and one rather expensive set of dining room chairs had been damaged beyond repair. The damage had been done by Singers leaning back in their chairs as they "partied." I had the damages added onto the rent bill...to keep it covered...and paid for the damages along with the rest of the items we owed money for.

The only real aspect about the conduct of the Singers which surprised me was that they were all personally handpicked by Richard Roberts. He made a point of letting some of us know that those Singers were *his* people, that *he* picked them personally, and that they weren't to take orders from anyone without *his* approval. Whatever Richard's criteria were for selecting Singers, I can only assume that he didn't stress conduct requirements strongly enough. Still, all of them came from the ORU student body and they should have already known what the expectations were.

Egos

Occasionally, a student or faculty member will forget that there are only two classes of people at ORU: Oral Roberts and everyone else. When that oversight becomes obvious to Oral, someone generally gets "zapped." While control of ORU supposedly rests with the Board of Regents, Oral once threatened to close the school if the Dean of the Graduate School of Theology was not fired. The Dean, Dr. R. O. Corvin, had experienced a number of disagreements with Oral Roberts relating to the manner in which the School of Theology should be run. There were also some disagreements about how much speaking in tongues was to be emphasized. While Dr. Corvin apparently had the ego to stand up to Oral, he didn't have the money to re-open the School of Theology if Oral closed it. And, of course, Oral won the battle. He's still there and Dr. Corvin is long gone.

Occasionally, someone will back Oral down for a while. Not long ago, Oral wanted to replace his current Chairman of the Board of Regents with another man. He had one of his associates approach the gentleman and find out what the reaction would be. The gentleman became upset with the idea that he might be replaced as Board Chairman and threatened to go with another evangelist, such as Billy Graham. Inasmuch as the Board Chairman was a millionaire and brought lots of money into the organization through informal channels, Oral decided to back off a while...until the waters had cooled and the timing was better. Within three years, the gentleman decided to retire and Oral immediately replaced him with the man he had in mind.

Oral's ego is derived from basic insecurity. Psychologists believe this to be a rather universal trait in the human species. The bigger the apparent ego, and the more it needs to be fed, the more you can believe that the person showing such an ego is actually suffering from a rather low self-concept which is derived from feelings of insecurity.

Oral Roberts reveals that type of ego just about every week of the year. One time we were going to tape students walking across campus (as they exited from chapel) for a television special. It was necessary that an announcement be made in Chapel, instructing all the students to act "normally" and not look at, or point to, the camera. Well, the chaplain, Rev. Bob

Stamps, got the jump on Oral and made the announcement himself. Oral became extremely upset about the matter and chewed on his producer after the Chapel. In attending to the necessary details, I had given instructions for the announcement to Oral's secretary *and* to the Chaplain's Office...just in case. I didn't want to have to tape the Chapel exit more than once, because we were also using aerial shots from a helicopter. Under such circumstances, logistics can become hairy. I didn't care *who* made the announcement in Chapel...I just wanted to make sure that whoever did make it knew what they were talking about when they gave instructions to the student body.

Well, Oral cared and he was close to being incensed that Bob Stamps had made the announcement instead of him. I asked the producer what difference it really made and he shrugged his shoulders and replied, "Well, Oral wanted to say it himself!" I reminisced a while after that incident and realized, of the people I knew who had been chewed out by Oral, they had been chewed on because they had somehow punctured Oral's ego...usually in what most of us would consider insignificant ways. While I never have been very good at "polishing the apple," I did decide after that incident to be more aware of possible circumstances that might cause Oral's ego to start "huffin' and puffin'."

We used a makeup artist on a couple of shows, including the special we taped in North Carolina, whose father is the most famous makeup artist in Hollywood. The son, also a good makeup artist, is a congenial type who is accustomed to being around, and working with, big stars everyday of his working life. That's his job...putting makeup on Hollywood movie and television stars. He's worked around them all his life and he isn't overwhelmed by them; he's natural, friendly, and open. Oral didn't like that. He wanted a makeup artist who acted more respectful around him. You might conclude that Oral even wanted his makeup man to "kowtow" just a little. The producer told me that the makeup artist might become a "problem" and I should be prepared to handle anything that came up. It did.

During a pre-production picnic which included Oral and Evelyn as guests, we were all seated around the huge set, eating Chicken Kiev and generally relaxing after a long week's work of getting ready for the taping. The makeup artist walked up to Oral and Evelyn and began talking to them. I kept a casual eye on Oral and began to notice that he was becoming upset. Almost immediately, the producer, who had also been keeping an eye on that conversation, came up to me and asked me, "Will you go get that makeup man out of there? Get him away from Oral!"

I casually walked up to the man and asked if I could talk with him a minute. We walked 30 to 40 yards away from the picnic area and I told him, "Look, I know you're used to being around lots of big stars and I also know that many of them look upon you as a friend. That man over there, though, is different. Oral doesn't want you for a friend. You make him up and keep your mouth shut. If he wants to have you for a friend, *he'll* choose *you*. But, you don't go to him. I don't know any other way to tell you this, but as far as he's concerned, you don't even exist other than when he wants you to make him up. Understand?"

The makeup artist replied, "Okay. That's cool. I understand." But, he was hurt and he had every right to be. In a few moments, the producer walked up to me and asked me what I said. I told him and *he* thought it was great! Later that evening, he told Oral what I had said to the makeup artist, and Oral also thought it was great!

Much later in the evening, a drunk tourist walked up to the set and began pestering Oral. I didn't have to be told what to do on that occasion. I collared the man and after I'd gotten him out of earshot, I told him to stay away from Oral or I'd bust his jaw in the name of the Lord!

After that, I became the unofficial "bouncer" for "the family" whenever we were on location tapings. G. B.

Sholes...writer, associate producer, and then bouncer. I had really made it to the top!

I later learned that Oral was very impressed with what he perceived to be my opinion of him. He interpreted my comments to the makeup artist to mean that I considered Oral to be a much bigger star than those in Hollywood...and while some of *them* might socialize with makeup artists, Oral certainly didn't. *Oh, well.*

Without going into great details and giving one example after another, I am sure that all of you know several people who would be much better humans if they could somehow control their egos. True, while it takes a well-developed self-concept for a man to drive himself to succeed, it seems counter-productive that the ego which often goes with self-concept reveals the successful person to be an eagle attempting to stay inside a thin shelled egg. And God help the man who cracks that shell. He gets himself clawed up by the eagle inside.

Over my lifetime, I've had the good fortune to work with and for some very talented people. In most cases, many of those people would have been able to go much, much further (because of their talent) if they'd simply been able to control their egos. Egos can damage and hurt. Egos can create poor impressions and bad reputations. If allowed to travel unchecked, egos can also get in the way of better judgment and even begin to cloud the process of rational thought. Hitler, Nixon, etc., are examples of that syndrome. And I'm not above believing that the evils of a man's ego can attack and bring down a man of God.

As stated at other times in this book, Oral Roberts is a complex human being. I have seen him in quiet, humble moods when he was personally hurting over something. On those occasions, I observed that he was personally hurting over other people's problems more than his own. There is no doubt in my mind that he has a tremendous capacity for sympathizing with the problems of humanity. Whenever observed him in that "mood," I was prepared to follow him *anywhere* and do anything I could to help him in his ministry. If he could stay *that way,* all the time, he'd never have any problems.

It's when he lets his insecurities roll over him and allows himself to strike back, revealing that enormous "insecurity-built" ego, that he begins to lose friends and support.

The ORU graduate

I watched several of them go through school, watched some of them graduate, and observed some of them go out into the real world looking for jobs. For some inexplicable reason, many of them seemed to want to remain on the ORU campus and work there. To be sure, there is a definite trend on the ORU campus to hire as many graduates as possible. In some ways that's good. Second and third line administrators are often more effective when they have a thorough understanding of the institution in which they're working. In another way, hiring too many employees who are graduates of an institution can be bad. It's called in-breeding in academic circles and many institutions try to avoid it. Some institutions don't even like graduate students to get their M.S. and Ph.D from the same school. They feel that a variety of academic input will better serve the graduate student than growing up intellectually in just one environment. One could conclude that the practice of doing it either way is a matter of opinion *or* is dictated by the availability of certain kinds of study at the graduate level in specialized areas. If an institution has the absolute best program in the country in Business Administration, for example, then any arguments that one shouldn't do graduate studies at that institution for a M.S. and a Ph.D. are weak. At this point, however, ORU doesn't have to worry about that kind of problem. ORU doesn't offer anything, yet.

If there is one thing about typical ORU graduates that disturbs me, it is their demonstrated inability, in general, to deal with the real world. Up front, I should state that there are exceptions...and some very good ones. But, I'm speaking of the general graduate who gets his degree from ORU. And, in over three years, I observed quite a few of them. Further, inasmuch as ORU is a rather small school, staff members get to know quite a few students while they're employed by the institution. During a typical taping of a special, for example, I have had as many as 50 students working for me as stage-hands, electricians, audio and lighting assistants, production assistants, etc. I got to know lots of them. And, from the amount of advice that some of them often came to me for, I assume that I might have even been viewed by some as sort of "surrogate father." I did have a lot of good, clean-cut, naive kids working for me on television specials and I enjoyed trying to help them whenever I could. Surprisingly to me, many of them seemed to have an inordinate number of hang-ups about religion. They'd say things like, "The devil's tempted me to do this or that," and some of the things they were talking about were absolutely normal for young people their age. In other words, many of them weren't at peace with either their religion or themselves. It was almost as if they didn't *really* want to live by all the rules which they perceived to be imposed on them by their religion.

Inner conflict, resulting from their inability to equate a successful life built around religious principles seemed very apparent. Some of them, because of working in television (and majoring in that subject), wanted to go to the West Coast to find work. However, they felt guilty about wanting to do that. Perhaps it wouldn't be the Lord's will to go out there and work in such a sinful environment. "Well," I'd shrug, "if your religion is working for you, it won't matter *what* environment you work in. You'll leave your mark with the people you're working around *through* the work you're doing. And while you'll inevitably have to join some kind of union on the Coast, there's nothing I know of in any of their union rules that states you'll have to smoke, drink, swear, or fornicate."

They'd reply, "But I've heard so many stories about things that go on out on the Coast." I'd respond with, "Well, you've probably heard some of those same type stories about people in Tulsa and on this campus." They'd smile knowingly and walk off with their conflicts still unresolved.

Perhaps the general aura of the "forbidden fruit" is what bothers the average ORU student so much after he or she graduates. There are some rather convincing arguments to the effect that if something tempts you, go ahead and do it! Then, make up your mind once and for all whether that temptation is something you do or don't like. In other words, once you've done that, you can settle the issue in your own mind and probably never be bothered by it again, one way or the other, for the rest of your life. You can then get on with whatever else you consider important in your life. Too many students at ORU, however, are insulated from...or more appropriately, excluded from...resolving such conflicts in the manner described above. The rules at ORU won't let them test their temptations. Instead of a temptation being tried and turned into either a personal practice or a non-entity, it remains a temptation. That's not good for anybody. If you're tempted to go get drunk, then *go get drunk* in a manner where you won't kill yourself finding out about how it feels. Once you've done that, you'll probably conclude, like 99% of the people do 99% of the time, that getting drunk is a waste of time, energy, booze, and aspirin.

It should be pointed out that the Pentecostal denominations which support Oral Roberts do not approve of the following: drinking, smoking, dancing, swearing, or any variation of adultery. Most "religious folks" would probably concur with these prohibitions...except for dancing and moderate social drinking. There really doesn't seem to be anything inherently wrong with dancing. Especially the kind of dancing which young folks do these days...standing about ten feet away from each other and individually gyrating to the beat of a different drummer. The Pentecostals imply, however, that dancing is a prelude to sexual activity and is, therefore, to be avoided. If I'd have known as a young man that dancing was a prelude to sex, I might have taken my jitterbug and twist more seriously! In my Presbyterian naivete, I guess I missed out on a lot of golden opportunities...as did most of the other young men and women of my generation!

Back to the point, student groups at ORU are not allowed to hold organized dances. Oral personally put the squelch on one dance that a group of students wanted to hold at Southern Hills Country Club in Tulsa. After living for four years under such restrictions, the graduates I've observed who remained in Tulsa seemed to then feel free to begin spending many of their evenings in the disco clubs in town. They couldn't dance as students but they *can* as graduates seems to be the attitude. None of it seemed to make much sense to me.

One ORU graduate who became an employee of Oral Roberts University married a young lady who had also graduated from ORU. Within a year they were divorced. While they were married, they lived a rather straight life. Once divorced, they both began doing things that normal young men and women do: they'd find a date and go out dancing. The young man I observed seemed to be preoccupied with the whole scene, however. I wouldn't have known about his activities if he hadn't talked so much about them. Nearly every time I observed him in my department, visiting with friends of his who worked for me, he'd be talking about where he'd gone dancing the night before. He'd describe the physical attributes of his date and brag about how far he'd gotten on the first night, etc. Promiscuous sexual activity seemed to have taken over his life. Now, this young man was not a teenager indulging in some verbalized sexual fantasy as high school boys are known to do in the locker room after gym class. This young man was in his mid-twenties, was a college graduate, had been married, and suddenly became consumed by his interest in sexual indulgence.

As a casual student of human nature, I was puzzled by his behavior. It seemed especially inappropriate inasmuch as he was both a graduate and an employee of Oral Roberts University. His relatively aberrant behavior was not as significant, however, as was his apparent need *to talk about it*. Through his actions and his conversations, he seemed to be saying, *"Well, I put up with ORU's rules for four years, but I'm out from under them now and I'm going to do everything I didn't get to do then, and I'm going to talk about it all I please!"* I initially judged this young man to be abnormal, based upon comparisons between him and other college graduates I had known on two other college campuses.

And then I started to follow the progress of other recent ORU graduates. I casually began to ask questions about how this or that recent ORU graduate was doing. The answers I began getting over the three years I was at ORU surprised me. As one would have reason to expect, several graduates did, indeed, go out into the world and begin leading productive lives. On the other hand, I heard accounts of what seemed to be an inordinate number of ORU graduates whose post-graduate lives were out of character with the ORU image.

The reported divorce rate among graduates seemed to be high. Reports of this or that person simply living with someone, rather than marrying them, were numerous. Stories of excessive drinking were a dime a dozen. Job-hopping seemed to come up quite often and it also became apparent that many ORU graduates went into lines of work that had nothing to do with their formal education.

Rather automatically, I began comparing what appeared to be an ORU Syndrome with past experiences I was familiar with in my own professional life. I onced worked in the alumni office of a large university which had well over one hundred thousand alumni. During my years there, I literally came to know thousands of alumni and students on that campus. That campus was a state university, not a religious institution. It had over 20,000 students, not 3,500 like ORU. If there *are* advantages which a small, religious institution would have over a large state university, then comparisons of former students from two such different campuses would certainly seem to fall in favor of the smaller school...especially in the area of observable aspects of Christian living.

Try as I might, and being as fair as I could in as many ways as possible, I came to this conclusion: graduates of that state university, in general, lead "straighter," more productive, more Christian lives than do graduates of Oral Roberts University! That is my personal observation after having worked at both institutions. Furthermore, using present-day measurements of "success," my observation is that the accomplishments of the state university's graduates *far* exceed those of Oral Roberts University.

The "Whole Man" concept of education for the body, mind, and spirit is a myth, a phrase, and a hook upon which ORU places its bait! Dustin Hoffman went to the wrong school! "The Graduate" should have been filmed in Tulsa, Oklahoma!

Chapter 6

ORAL: The Man, the Mystery, the Millionaire

Oral's background

Oral Roberts' background is fairly well-known by most of his followers. He loves to tell how he came from meager beginnings: "When I was a child, we didn't live at the end of the world, but you could see it from our back porch!" Or, when he talks about how poor his parents were, he says, "Even the poor folks called *us* poor!"

All of that appears to be true. The pictures which Oral shows of himself as a youngster look as if he lived his early years in impoverished squalor. That kind of a start in life can leave an indelible impression on a young man's mind when he compares himself with the rest of the world and how it lives. Oral has often stated that he and his brother rebelled against the poverty they lived in and blamed it on God...or blamed it on their parents for working for God as ministers.

All of us have known poor people. Some of us have even been poor ourselves. Not many of us, however, have hated our existence so much or been so ashamed of our parents that it caused us to move away from our own parents at age sixteen and move in with someone else. Oral Roberts did. He moved from Ada to the nearby town of Atoka and moved in with a judge. Access to the judge's law books may have been what sparked Oral's expressed interest in law or perhaps someday..."becoming governor of Oklahoma."

Oral never became Governor of Oklahoma, but he has known a few of them. Governor Hall of Oklahoma, before going to jail for fraud, had a cottage reserved for him in Oral's retirement center. It was cottage number 19 and it was the only cottage at that time that had a bomb shelter in it. The cottage was reserved for the Governor's use whenever he was in Tulsa. The cottage was still reserved for the Governor...even after he was sent to prison...as late as March 1978.

Today, Oral isn't poor anymore. His house in Tulsa has been estimated to be valued in the neighborhood of $250,000. He also purchased a home in Palm Springs that has been valued at one million dollars by Thunderbird Development Corporation. Membership at the Thunderbird Country Club to which Oral and Richard belong, bears a price tag of $25,000 today.

Oral Roberts wears expensive clothes today...nothing like the pictures he has shown of himself as a child. Today, he wears Brioni suits on his television shows and the price of a Brioni ranges from $500 to $1,000. Those are pretty nice "threads" for a man who loves to talk about his meager beginnings.

Oral Roberts flies around the country in a $2 million fanjet falcon. Flight records show that in the period from July 1978 through June 1979 he flew out of Tulsa on an average of once every two weeks, usually to Palm Springs. The plane is used almost exclusively by Oral, often for trips that have nothing to do with Association business.

Oral Roberts also experienced health problems as a young man. In addition to being a stutterer, he also tells us that he had tuberculosis. And while Oral occasionally stutters, even today, no hard evidence has ever been produced to verify that he ever *really* did have tuberculosis. By Oral's own account in his book, *My Story,* doctors diagnosed his illness at age seventeen as tuberculosis. After he was supposedly miraculously healed, actual sputum tests were taken and sent to the State Hospital in Oklahoma City...with negative reports. A fluoroscope test taken after his recovery also showed his lungs to be clear. Sputum records are kept by the State Hospital in Oklahoma City for only five years...and, even then, the patient's records can only be released with the patient's permission. Today, only Oral Roberts could produce hard evidence that he ever did, indeed, really have tuberculosis.

The point is this: no sputum tests or fluoroscope tests were apparently taken *before* Oral's diagnosis of tuberculosis. Those tests were taken *after* his "miraculous healing" to prove that he did *not* have tuberculosis. His own accounts of his healing have tended to vary over the years. In his book, *My Story,* Oral indicated that he began hemorrhaging from tuberculosis before his seventeenth birthday in the last moments of a basketball game. Oral's birthday is January 24, so one can assume that this basketball game was in the middle of the basketball season...probably sometime in January of 1935. Oral has in the past always maintained that he was healed instantly. In fact, within a few weeks after his miraculous recovery, he was ordained in the Pentecostal Holiness Church and began conducting summer revival meetings. By the end of the summer of 1938, he was also holding evangelistic meetings with his father. His past stories and autobiographies have always indicated that he was instantly healed.

However, after Oral announced plans to build the City of Faith in 1978, he began to tell a variation of that story. He stated on several TV programs (after the City of Faith announcement) that it took him over a year to recuperate from his illness. His message on those programs implied that it took prayer *and* medicine to heal him of tuberculosis...a variation of the story that fits in rather well with the role which the City of Faith is supposed to play in the delivery of holistic health care! In other words, as late as 1961, Oral was stating that tests taken within two months after his healing indicated that his lungs were absolutely clear of TB. In 1978, however, he stated on television that it took over a year for his total healing to occur. Which story is true? No one really knows but Oral!

Oral has also indicated that he was healed of his stuttering at the same time he was healed of tuberculosis. However, Oral Roberts still stutters occasionally, and there are several words which give him problems. While no one would be justified in criticizing Oral for stuttering, one wonders why he says that God healed him of stuttering when in fact he still stutters. Many people don't realize Oral still stammers. The typical viewer of one of Oral Roberts' telecasts has no way of realizing or detecting the number of edits that were made in order to remove words that Oral had muffed during one of his sermons or during one of those typical "impromptu" conversations that he often had with guests on his shows.

The electronics of television make it possible to "remove" words that are spoken (for either time, content, or quality reasons) and only a highly experienced person in television will detect such edits. The average viewer never notices such edits.

In working rather closely with Oral for over three years, I noticed that he seemed to stutter more when he was either tired or under stress. And then, there were times when he didn't stutter at all...such as when he was in a good mood or when he seemed totally comfortable with either his activity, his environment, or his human company. However, if he was subjected to a stress-filled situation, his stammering would return. During long conversations that might touch upon many topics, I found that subjects which did not annoy him (for which he had answers off the top of his head) produced no stammering...he would not stutter at all. When the topic changed to something that irritated or perplexed him, he would begin stammering again. I found this interesting, even intriguing at times.

Interestingly enough, Oral is very comfortable in front of a live audience and seldom stutters when giving a sermon to such a group. Inasmuch as he is something of a natural showman, I concluded that he enjoys using his considerable powers of persuasion on a large audience...and feels so comfortable in that situation that he experiences no stress whatsoever, revealing little or no inclination to stammer.

On the other hand, the relatively foreign environment of a television production set...where cameras, cameramen, audio men, and lighting men all have a hand in determining how well he "comes off"...apparently causes Oral to feel uncertain and ill at ease. Even with a live audience for him to relate to on a production set, he will stammer. In general, I've never seen Oral as at ease on a television production set as he is in front of a live audience where no cameras are present.

The simple point is that Oral still occasionally stammers in spite of his claim that he was healed of tuberculosis and stuttering at the same time. When I first heard Oral Roberts speak to a large tent congregation in 1954, he did not stutter. When I first heard him speak on a television production set in 1975, he *did* stutter. After many hours of observing Oral during television productions, I wonder whether Oral may not have a deeply seated sense of inferiority or insecurity...whenever he is subjected to stress or uncertainty, his stammering becomes noticeable. In that context consider too the following statement Oral Roberts made in his book *The Call* in 1972:

"Yet, despite how much every person wants to be accepted by the establishment and leaders of the nation, I have known deep within that this could never be for me."

That statement by Oral reveals a rather laid-back inferiority complex. Other evidence tends to indicate that Oral does suffer from some feelings of inferiority. One incident which I remember from my days as an Oral Roberts' employee related to the way in which Oral reacted to the way someone had treated him. His reactions against the individual had been angry, mean, and petty. One official, a vice-president for Oral, remarked to me, "I wish Oral *wouldn't act* that way. He's still trying to claw his way up. He doesn't have to *do* that, today. He has all this money, all this power, and a university named after him, but, when he gets cornered, he starts clawing all over again."

Interested, I asked the official, "Is it because of his background?" He replied, "Of course! But he doesn't have to *be* that way, any more!" *But, he is.* Another statement made to me about Oral Roberts, shortly after I had arrived on the campus, tends to corroborate the inferiority complex theory. Oral's closest associate warned me, in the process of telling me how I'd have to act in getting along with Oral as a writer, that I shouldn't attempt to become too friendly with HIM. The associate told me, "There are two classes of people on this campus: Oral Roberts *and then everyone else.* And as long as you don't ever forget that, you'll get along with him alright." I've always found it interesting...the people who are secure in themselves seldom feel the need to put others down. Unfortunately, this does *not* describe Oral.

I never forgot that and I never had any problems with the man. Some who *did* forget it left Oral Roberts University rather quickly. More about that later.

Oral's motivations

Oral Roberts' disclosures about his background tell of poverty, sickness, and unhappiness during his early years. He has clearly stated that the reason he left his parents' home at the age of sixteen was to get away from them, their religion, their discipline, and their poverty.

Everything Oral Roberts has done since that departure from home has been an effort toward achieving recognition. And it began when he jumped out of his chair at the age of seventeen and ran around the evangelist's platform screaming, "I am healed, I am healed!"

Oral Roberts *wants and needs* recognition. One vice-president told me a story about Oral's wishes to have a "founder's room" established in the Learning Resources Center at Oral

Roberts University. The VP went to Oral several times with various suggestions as to what should be in the founder's room. The VP proposed to Oral that large portraits of various regents be placed in the room, lining the walls. Oral kept replying that it didn't sound quite right. "Work on it some more," he said.

Finally the VP figured it out. He ordered the biggest portrait of Oral Roberts that he could find, had it installed on the wall of the founder's room, and waited for Oral's reactions. Oral never said a word about the founder's room to the VP again. The VP did what he was supposed to...he put the picture of the founder in the founder's room!

On several occasions while working for Oral Roberts, his closest associate asked me to endeavor to get Oral on the Johnny Carson show, the Dinah Show, the Tomorrow Show, the Jerry Lewis Telethon, and others. The associate would always give me dates on which Oral Roberts could be out of Tulsa and available for personal appearances on such network shows which were aired out of Hollywood. Then, the associate would always caution me, "Don't call me back and tell me that you've arranged an invitation for Oral to be on this or that show. Instead, have one of *their* people call and have *them* ask if he can appear."

I replied, "What's the difference?" He responded, "There's a big difference. He wants to hear it from *them!*"

And, so, I'd get on the phone and begin calling this or that producer on the West Coast, endeavoring to wangle an appearance by Oral Roberts. I always did it right, too. I *always* had one of them call Oral's office and extend a personal invitation.

On other occasions, the titles of some of Oral's quarterly prime time television shows would be changed...in order to make Oral's name appear more conspicuously. When we went to Alaska in 1975 to tape a special there, the name of the show was changed from "IN ALASKA WITH ORAL ROBERTS" to "ORAL ROBERTS IN ALASKA." *First things first!*

Oral's personality

I never did figure out, to my own satisfaction, what Oral Roberts' true personality actually is. He shows many different faces to many different people. His television personality is one face which millions see. That particular face seems to be filled with kindness, concern for the problems of his fellowmen, and a genuine desire to help everyone get ahead. He can walk onto a TV set and turn on that charm, and then walk offstage while Richard is singing and absolutely lacerate his producer for something he didn't like. And when Oral tells someone "off," he does it so they *really know* they've been chewed on. For example, during one show segment when we were taping the Alaska special, the noise of a still camera was being picked up on Oral's mike and recorded on videotape. The still camera was being operated by one of Oral's permanent employees... who, incidentally, had been with Oral Roberts for years. Anyway, when the technical director realized that the sound of the shutter clicking had been recorded on videotape, he told the producer that the segment would have to be taped over again...without the noise. It was a very short segment and shouldn't have caused any concern at all. In Hollywood, several "takes" are often recorded just for safety. But, when the producer told Oral that he would have to do the segment over again, Oral became upset and wanted to know why. When the producer told Oral *why* the segment needed to be re-taped, Oral stated, "Well, *he's* one of our *own* men. Just go over there and break both of his legs!" Perhaps Oral didn't know it, but that entire conversation was being recorded on videotape and the entire crew later listened to it. Obviously, Oral's comment didn't go over very well with a television crew that had lived on two to four hours sleep for nearly two weeks...trying to give Oral Roberts the best possible show they could! And here was Oral Roberts, for a moment sounding like a mobland gangster. And while that comment was never included in the edited version of the show, it is on file in the tape library at Oral Roberts University.

Oral has a capability for "reading" people and he sizes them up rather quickly. In a one-on-one situation where he is attempting to influence someone, the personality he shows will depend upon how he sizes the person up. For example, his personality around guest stars has been noticeably different on various occasions...depending upon who the guest star was that was appearing on his show. When Jerry Lewis was a guest on Oral's show, Oral would scold Jerry for smoking and would not allow Jerry to smoke around him or around the set. Oral told Jerry, "Why don't you stop putting that trash into your lungs?" Jerry acquiesced on that point, and inasmuch as Jerry Lewis is a chain smoker, he had quite a time working with Oral and then running completely off the set to grab a cigarette...out of the range of Oral's nose! Oral dominated Jerry Lewis whenever they were together. And while Jerry made quite a few humorous comments about not being able to smoke around Oral, he did bow to Oral's wishes.

On the other hand, a certain lady with a lot of character and lots of spine by the name of Dionne Warwick sat backstage during a Christmas show taping and smoked right beside Oral. And she did it while Richard was out on the set singing an extremely religious song! Oral didn't say a word. She had *him* spooked! Dionne has a strong personality, is very talented, and is also very sure of herself. If Oral had said anything, she probably would have walked off his set...and Oral probably knew it! But, he needed her for his Christmas show and, so, he tolerated her cigarette smoking...but he wouldn't let Jerry Lewis get by with it!

As another example, Oral is usually very forceful around Richard. He tends to try to dominate Richard. After all, Richard is his son. Richard, however, has a backbone of his own, and when he gets his dander up, the fur can fly! On one occasion, Richard actually backed Oral off. The story follows:

Oral had gotten extremely upset with Richard's wife, Patti, and they had gotten into some strong words. Richard had concluded that Patti was right, but Oral wouldn't back down from Patti and admit he was wrong. Further, he wouldn't forgive Patti for disagreeing with him. Well, Richard got Oral onto a half-hour program one day and read Oral a scripture to the effect "that a man who does not know forgiveness in his heart cannot know God."

That shook Oral noticeably and while the things "between the lines" on the show were not apparent to the television audience, it was very apparent to some of us who knew the circumstances. Oral was actually moved emotionally and told Richard on the show that the scripture made him realize that *HE* had to think. The two of them held hands and prayed together and it turned out to be a rather good half-hour program.

Later, however, Oral got upset with Patti again and made a comment, "I'm not about to let some *skirt* tell *me* how to run this ministry." Shortly thereafter, Patti resigned from her television responsibilities and began her own ministry of song and sermon. I actually think that if Patti and Richard had been able to live their own lives without being in the goldfish bowl called Oral Roberts Ministries, their marriage would not have ended in divorce. Patti has her own mind, her own will-power, and she was never really allowed to "do her thing" around Oral Roberts. Richard went to bat for her several times, but it didn't work out. If there was ever anything I admired about Richard Roberts, it was his own tenacity in trying to make his marriage work. And if blame is to be assessed for that marriage not working, some of it has to fall on Oral.

Oral's temperament

Oral Roberts has been known to go into a blind rage. And when he does, Evelyn hides the car keys from him so he can't get into his car and go off speeding down the hill in his high-powered Seville or Mercedes. The last time she had to do that was when the Oklahoma Health Systems Agency reached a decision that upset Oral Roberts regarding the City of Faith.

He got so mad in a vice-president's office one time that he reached across the man's desk and threw a coffee cup against the wall! Tsk, tsk, "Be like Jesus, Oral."

Rather recently he got so upset in the office of one of Governor Nigh's aides that he became unable to speak, began crying and screaming, and made a statement to the effect that he didn't know if he'd be able to pull the deal off or not. *He was talking about the City of Faith.*

Tricks of the trade

Oral Roberts *does* have a certain magnetism about him. People don't really know what to expect when they meet him personally and he takes advantage of that uncertainty to his benefit.

My first exposure to him was when I met with him and his producer to discuss the summer special that was taped and aired in 1975. When the producer introduced me to Oral Roberts I offered my hand in response to his outstretched hand and I expected a strong, hearty handshake. After all, Oral Roberts is 6'2" and I took his hand and I *squeezed* it! At least, I squeezed it for a split second. What I had in *my* hand, the hand of Oral Roberts, was a limp piece of flesh! He didn't squeeze in the normal fashion of a handshake at all. He merely stuck out his hand, placid and limp, and I heard and felt the bones of his knuckles scrape together when I bore down. But, *he* didn't flinch. *I did!* I thought, *"Oh, my God, I've broken his hand!"*

While I didn't break any bones in his hand, the experience temporarily rattled me. That gave him an immediate advantage and he began asking me questions about the upcoming show, theme path, points to emphasize, etc. Within a few minutes; I realized he'd pulled that limp-handed business on purpose to gain an upper hand during our initial meeting. If you think I'm kidding about the effect that has, *you* try it the next time you're trying to impress someone you're meeting for the first time. Give them a limp hand; don't flinch when they nearly break your knuckles and then begin acting mysterious; ask pointed questions and stare thoughtfully. You'll have your man on the defensive immediately, I assure you! It was a good trick and I grinned about it as I walked down the hall away from my first meeting with Oral Roberts.

With most people, including the stars who appear on his television shows, Oral nearly always endeavors to retain a certain air of aloofness. He likes to work with outside people *through his own people.* In other words, you don't often get to deal directly with the president, you deal with one of his aides. His deliberate air of mysterious aloofness absolutely overwhelmed Robert Goulet when he was on Oral's set for a Christmas show. In fact, Goulet was so awed that he could hardly talk to Oral during the segment of the show when they were *supposed* to talk. It was a very short talk session and Goulet almost immediately went into his second number.

Money, power, and the need for recognition

Oral has always favored doing things on a grand scale. An ordinary church wasn't big enough for him, probably because the congregation of an ordinary church wouldn't be big enough for him. Oral has stated that when he does something for God, he tries to do it first class. And he began doing it up in first class fashion as far back as the mid-fifties.

In 1955, Oral's personal salary was reportedly $25,000 when he was still holding those huge tent revivals. He accepted one love offering out of six in each campaign and that increased his income to $65,000. That same year, royalties from his books netted him another $80,000, totalling a combined income of $145,000 for the year.

That same year, 1955, the Healing Waters Corporation took in $3,000,000 through the mails and netted a profit of $150,000 from a full-length film, "Ventures Into Faith."

Now that's a lot of money today and it was a terrific sum back in the mid-fifties!

That much money brought power with it and Oral soon began to enjoy some of its fruits, including investiture as a board member of the National Bank Corporation. When that much money brings power, it also brings political clout...and political clout *always* helps when you attempt to deal with the federal government. In the mid-sixties, when over 200 private colleges across the country were having severe financial problems, Oral Roberts University somehow received a federal construction loan for $2,985,000. And in 1965, Oral Roberts University received an outright grant of $520,000 *from the taxpayers* under Title I of the Higher Education Act. However, Oral Roberts has told seminar guests visiting the university that "this institution will follow God's way" because ORU doesn't have to worry about outside controls that come along with the receipt of federal funds!

On April 2, 1967, Oral Roberts got the recognition he so desperately wanted. On that day, Oral Roberts University was dedicated and Billy Graham served as the speaker...in front of an audience numbering in the thousands. On that day, Oral Roberts was also named president of Oral Roberts University and assumed a title which most academicians would consider a non de plume for him..."Dr." Oral Roberts.

Using people

Anyone who goes as far as Oral Roberts has, by necessity, had to use other people to help him achieve his goals. What I've seen is that if someone can help him, Oral courts them; if they can't, he ignores them.

The Reverend Steve Pringle was the first person Oral Roberts really used to his advantage. Reverend Pringle allowed Oral Roberts to take over his revival tent for a week...and the meetings became so successful that the revival was continued for over a month. During that time, a man with a revolver fired into the tent while the meeting was underway. The police arrested the man and later released him...which seems rather odd...and the story was picked up by wire services and was seen in newspapers all over the country. Oral claimed after the incident that it made him, overnight, a controversial evangelist. You could almost conclude that Oral Roberts owed his success, and his tent meeting style, to the Reverend Steve Pringle. Steve Pringle's name is *never* mentioned in any of Oral Roberts' books. How's that for gratitude?

An elderly man who had spent years as a geologist collecting precious and semi-precious stones, jewels, and rocks retired at University Village...the final development arm of the Oral Roberts Ministries. The man wished to retire at University Village and he offered to donate his collection to the Oral Roberts Association if he could, in turn, be allowed to display his collection in the Village while he lived there. The collection is an amazing example of rare stones and other pieces of geological interest showing the beauty in God's kingdom. The Tulsa papers ran an article about the collection, complete with pictures, and created quite an interest in the exhibit, valued at several hundred thousand dollars.

The elderly gentleman extended a personal invitation to Oral Roberts to come for a private tour of the collection. The man didn't want any publicity...he just wanted to show Oral the collection that he was going to leave him when he died. Oral Roberts' office did not respond to the invitation. Others were extended through the Village administrator's office via a vice-president who is Oral's closest associate. Still no answer. The old gentleman became rather upset and, finally, Evelyn Roberts visited the retiree and viewed the collection herself to smooth things over.

Oral Roberts used the man's wishes to leave part of his estate to a tax exempt entity and, through the publicity which the man's collection attracted, gained some goodwill for the retirement center throughout the community. Oral's indifference, however, to the man's personal wishes for a short, private audience seems callous and out of character...not quite like a man who had "spent a lifetime" planting seeds of faith and hope in other people's lives.

According to Oral Roberts, the idea of Seed-Faith occurred to him as he was driving down the highway, viewing crops being harvested in the fall. He later wrote a book entitled *Miracle of Seed-Faith* and he gave it away by the millions, exceeding the circulation of all previous books that he had written. The concept of Seed-Faith is also to be found in a magazine, *Chimes,* which tends to be a little on the far-out side. Who came up with Seed-Faith first...Oral or *Chimes?* Who knows? It did work for Oral so well, however, that it turned his ministry around. Oral Roberts University was borrowing money for its payroll in 1968. In 1970, when *Miracle of Seed-Faith* came out, the money began pouring in again...and up through 1978, it appeared as if Oral's ministry was running in high gear.

Oral Roberts has used people and ideas which he judged would be useful to him in furthering his ministry. Webster's defines "eclecticism" as..."method or practice of selecting what seems best from various systems, especially in forming religious or philosophical doctrine...."

While Oral Roberts has been called "the High Priest of Faith Healing," we could also call him the Arch-Bishop of Evangelical Eclecticism!

Chapter 7

Basketball Bingo:
Playing to Win

Oral Roberts realized in the early days of Oral Roberts University that something would have to be done to keep it from becoming just another religious college, existing in obscurity somewhere in south Tulsa. Since it takes both time and a prominent, established faculty to develop a reputation for academic excellence, something other than an academic thrust would have to be attempted in order to keep the name of Oral Roberts University in the public eye.

The need for recognition

A successful athletic program is a sine qua non for any college or university in Oklahoma. For example, the University of Oklahoma's prestige within the state depends more upon the success of its football teams than it does upon the strength of its academic programs. Alumni, parents of students, and "supporters of higher education" in Oklahoma flock by the thousands to watch OU football and they usually know all the coaches' and football players' names. The great majority of that crowd wouldn't know the name of the president of the University of Oklahoma, however, and couldn't care less who was Dean of this or that college within the university. In short, in Oklahoma college and university reputations depend more upon prominence in sports than on academic excellence.

Oral Roberts, operating within that kind of environment in Oklahoma, knew he had to come up with something other than the phrase of "educating the whole man" if he was going to attract popular support and interest in Oral Roberts University. Inasmuch as he couldn't hope to mount a football team that would successfully compete with the University of Oklahoma, he had to come up with something else that would attract attention to ORU, not cost too much money, and also allow his school to develop a winning tradition. His entry into independent, non-conference basketball was an ideal way to achieve that goal.

There are literally hundreds of independent colleges in the U.S. which have varsity basketball teams that are little better than intramural teams at larger institutions. And the notable exceptions to that athletic reality were not the teams which Oral Roberts University scheduled its team to play in the early days of ORU basketball. The independent field was "ripe" for someone to enter and "clean up." And Oral Roberts began to do just that when he brought Ken Trickey in as head basketball coach at Oral Roberts University. When Ken Trickey left Middle Tennessee State University to go to ORU, he took several good players with him.

The team developed a style of "runnin' and gunnin'" and the fans began to enjoy going to ORU to watch a local team give some "home cooking" to opponents, often by margins of 30-40 points. In addition to the fun of watching a local team win big, fans also enjoyed listening to a pep band that played some *good* music and conveyed a created atmosphere of winning and clean-cut athletic Christianity in action.

The response from the Tulsa community was exactly what Oral Roberts had hoped for. Through its basketball team, ORU demonstrated that it could be a religious institution filled with freshly-scrubbed, clean-cut students, and still win big in college athletics. The fact that ORU opponents were obscure teams took a backseat to fans who saw dribbling, flashy passing, and a good assortment of fancy shots accented by more than an occasional slam dunk! In comparison to the teams which ORU booked in those days, Ken Trickey's team looked professional. The fast-break styles, augmented by a professional sounding pep band, got fans to talking. Other sports fans in Tulsa began buying season tickets and the press began covering ORU games regularly. It was *really* fun to watch the ORU Titans knock off Brown University, for example, by a 40-point margin and score over 100 points in the process.

In a rather short time, Tulsa University, in the highly competitive Missouri Valley Conference, found itself with another team in town that was competing for attention from fans and the press. And, naturally, it wasn't long before fans and sportswriters in Tulsa began to suggest that ORU and TU engage in an inter-city non-conference rivalry. That's exactly what Oral Roberts wanted: to beat the other basketball team in town.

Christianity vs. winning

One of the understated realities of winning in athletics follows: it isn't always possible to recruit good basketball players who are also "Christians." Most often, in order to attract good players to the ORU campus, some sort of compensation had to be provided which made up for the constraints which were imposed upon a basketball player's lifestyle at ORU. While few basketball players are given to either smoking or drinking, other aspects of life on the ORU campus can tend to make it less attractive than other campuses which also recruit basketball players. For example, not many campuses with basketball teams require their students to wear ties to class. Neither do they require their students to attend Chapel twice weekly. And seldom do other campuses necessarily require students to take courses in theology or the Holy Spirit. To make up for these disadvantages, ORU had to sweeten the pot so that its campus became attractive to potential players in other ways.

And while very few college campuses the size of Oral Roberts University have separate dormitories for athletes, ORU built one for obvious reasons. An athletic dormitory that had a recreational area, larger rooms than other students have, and luxurious surroundings made the environment at ORU relatively more attractive than it often is at other campuses similar in size. Equally important to Oral Roberts, an athletic dormitory isolated the athletes from other students...and any "Christian shortcomings" the athletes might reveal would not be all that obvious to other students.

Isolation from the general student body and relatively luxurious surroundings were important to Oral Roberts and his basketball players. One ardent Titan fan, who was also the son of one ORU vice-president, revealed that several of the ORU basketball players had smoked pot in their rooms in the athletic dormitory. This could not have been possible had the athletes been housed in pairs with other students in regular dorm facilities. By isolating athletes in their own dormitory, however, the situation as set up at ORU enabled athletes to engage in such indiscretions and, at the same time, keep the knowledge of such activities hidden from the overall student population at Oral Roberts University.

Other "goodies" that make life more attractive for ORU basketball players have materialized. More than one player drove a shiny new car while at ORU. Where did these come from? I was told that loans were sometimes cosigned which made it possible for a basketball player to "buy" a car. How one ORU player got the money to make the payments on a Continental Mark IV is not known. In one case, however, where an ORU basketball player got himself shot in Las Vegas (shortly after leaving ORU), the bank which had approved a co-signed loan called an ORU official and re-quested that something be done to arrange for continued pay-ments on the car which had been purchased through such means. The ORU official arranged to have a rather large sum of money put on deposit with the bank and it was left there for some time...the interest of which was retained by the bank as a method of continued payment on the Continental. I asked the ORU official (who'd made the arrangement) if he planned to have the car brought back to Tulsa. He replied, "No way! That car can *stay* in Las Vegas until it rusts!"

Such financial arrangements are apparently made through utilization of nominee accounts which are administered by either banks or attorneys. The use of such financing makes it difficult, if not impossible, to trace the money back to the ORU campus in any way.

Jobs without working

Recent NCAA investigations into the basketball program at ORU have turned up little. The NCAA, however, exhibits a surprising ignorance when it comes to knowing which rocks to look under. For example, it is against NCAA regulations for athletes or athletes wives to be put on the payroll *if they aren't actually working*.

If the NCAA, in investigating the basketball program at ORU, had taken the time to compare payroll records against personnel records, they would have found at least one star basketball player's wife on the payroll who was not listed by the personnel office as occupying *any* job slot on campus. One wonders if the NCAA is really that naive (or incompetent) in its investigation procedures when it fails to look for such infractions of NCAA rules. In any event, it appears as if the NCAA's investigation of Oral Roberts University's basketball program was incomplete!

The pressure to win

One might conclude that the NCAA views the possible improprieties of ORU recruiting a small matter in comparison with some of the other problems which the NCAA faces. Coaches of Oral Roberts University, however, would probably tend to view the matter a little differently. The pressure to win in basketball at Oral Roberts University doesn't come from its alumni, its students, or from the Tulsa community. The *real* pressure to win at ORU comes from the institution's president, Oral Roberts himself. And while very few college presidents involve themselves in recruiting basketball players, Oral Roberts has. One coach made the remark that Oral Roberts was the chief recruiter for the institution, not he. It is the kind of pressure that results from that intense an interest that undoubtedly contributed to the temptation to improperties.

Back in the early days of basketball at ORU, evidence of NCAA-rule violations was more apparent than it is today. With the success of the basketball program…and the visibility which came along with it…it became necessary to "clean up the act" somewhat. In addition to that, other subtle pressures were put on coaches to attempt to recruit better white players. For years, the basketball team at Oral Roberts University represented the majority of the black population on the campus. And as community interest in the program grew, so did the usual pressures which result in subtle hints that some good white players be recruited. That put lots of pressure on ORU coaches. In general, there are more good black basketball players in the country than there are white players. If you disagree with that statement, take a look at the pro ranks in basketball and start counting. The very simple truth of the matter is that there are more good black basketball players than white, *period*. Whether it is a result of natural ability or mere inclination is not proven. But, the headcount speaks for itself.

Back to the point, the pressure to recruit white players at ORU...once the program was successful...made at least two ORU coaches' lives uncomfortable. The white blue-chip basketball players who do come up through the high school ranks are *heavily* recruited by the best schools in the country and it is very evident that ORU will never be successful in recruiting that kind of white talent. On the other hand, the abundance of black basketball talent has made it rather easy for ORU to recruit black players.

And while Oral Roberts gave early ORU coaches the simple mandate of winning, the codicils which he added to his desires as the program progressed have made it increasingly difficult for an ORU coach to keep Oral happy. First, Oral merely wanted his ORU teams to win, then he wanted them to get invited to NIT and NCAA tournaments, and then he began to want his teams to win with the use of more white players. And finally, as it became apparent that the NCAA might begin looking into things at ORU, Oral decided that somehow his coach should win, win white, get invited to national tournaments, and still win honestly.

It should be pointed out that neither Jerry Hale nor Lake Kelly got themselves involved in any "deals." If any deals were made in recruiting players at ORU, they were made by other administrators on the campus. And while those administrators may feel fortunate that I'll leave them unnamed, I wish to make the point that the only reason for my comments along this line are to make it clear that neither of the above coaches are culpable when it comes to NCAA rules infractions.

Both of the above coaches, however, felt the kinds of pressures which have been mentioned. They had to win clean, win as white as possible, and by winning 20 or more games per season, hopefully get their teams invited to at least an NIT tournament. All those constraints added up on the ORU campus to make it exceedingly difficult for any coach. It is rather well-known in the Tulsa sports community that both

Jerry Hale and Lake Kelly left ORU because they couldn't do everything Oral Roberts wanted them to under his expanded set of rules. Further, it is rather revealing to know that one of the reasons Oral was displeased with Coach Lake Kelly was that, in disciplining certain of his athletes, he did so publicly. Oral didn't want that at all. He didn't want disciplinary problems with athletes at ORU to be a matter of public record. The implications of such public disciplinary reprimands would tend to suggest openly that perhaps all the athletes at ORU were not the epitome of Christianity. And, as everyone who's worked for Oral Roberts knows, he doesn't like that sort of thing, at all. And while *he* may know it, he doesn't want the general public to get wind of it.

If there is one thing about Oral Roberts which works against him, it is his inability to ever be satisfied. He personally should have remained contented with merely winning 20 games or more per season. That goal was proven to be compatible with the size and scope of his institution. It wasn't enough, however. Oral has publicly stated that he wants the ORU Titans to be capable of beating teams like UCLA three out of four times. Most sportswriters, fans, and university administrators across the country would agree that such a goal for Oral Roberts University is unrealistic.

The fantastic offer

As unrealistic as a "big league" basketball team may be for a school like ORU, the importance which Oral, himself, attaches to having a winning basketball team is best revealed by relating this authorized story from one of the country's leading universities.

On April 1, 1979 an ORU representative approached the basketball coach of a university team that had reached the quarter-finals of the 1979 NCAA Basketball Tournament. This coach was heading up one of the "sweet sixteen" teams in the country...among the best in the nation. The coach was reportedly stunned *at being offered two and one-half million dollars to take over the head coaching job at ORU.*

The above sum was to be paid over a ten-year period at $250,000 per year. The payment was to come from three sources: 1) from an automobile dealer in Tulsa, 2) from one of Oral's partners, and finally, 3) $100,000 from ORU. If the coach didn't accomplish everything Oral wanted him to...and didn't last the full ten years...he would still be paid the full two and one-half million dollars.

The coach...whom all basketball fans would recognize if named...turned down Oral's rather amazing offer and immediately reported it to his athletic director who, in turn, authorized the use of this information for publication in this book. It sort of makes you wonder if the half-million people who sent Oral $5.00 each realized that the money they contributed was about to make "something good" happen to Oral's basketball team!

And while it was well-known in Tulsa that Oral Roberts was irritated that his 1978-79 team did not earn a tournament bid, the turn-down by the above coach did not discourage Oral in the least. With the persistence of a razorback himself, Oral pursued the matter and three days later it was announced that ORU had hired Ken Hayes...whose team had also earned an invitation to the NCAA Basketball Championship Tournament!

Oral's "university" needs to have a winning basketball team...regardless of what it costs. Apparently, Oral thinks he can have a championship team only if he has a good, well-paid, head coach.

Chapter 8

The Pinoak Plunder:
A Royal Payoff in Royalties

Oral Roberts likes to project himself as a college president who lives on a rather modest income. Comparatively, his reported stipend as president of Oral Roberts University is not out of line and his reported $30,000 salary falls into an acceptable range which would not cause many eyebrows to raise at all.

What he *doesn't* like to talk about, however, are his other sources of revenue which make that $30,000 look like one tiny drop in a huge bucket. By virtue of his ex-cathedra position as head of all the Oral Roberts Enterprises, he maintains control over a financial empire that makes ordinary millionaires seem puny. He personally keeps a hand in everything that involves fund-raising within his organizations, and you find his personal touch in that area of involvement more than any other in his ministry. As will be revealed below, fund-raising also involves the books he gives away...because the more he has given away, the more he has made in royalties, through Pinoak Publications.

The numbers

As far back as 1955, Oral Roberts' personal annual income from royalties on his books was $80,000...and that figure was reported in a 1956 issue of *American* magazine, in an article entitled "King of the Faith Healers."

The copyright for Oral's books has been held by various corporate entities over the years, *or* by Oral Roberts, personally. Generally, the copyright has been held by the Oral Roberts Evangelistic Association, Tulsa, Oklahoma. As the head of a non-profit religious organization, that is the customary way a man in Oral's position would handle copyright and all the legal issues that are part and parcel of copyright laws.

On some of Oral's books, however, the inside cover shows that the copyright was retained by Oral Roberts. Not Oral Roberts Evangelistic Association or Oral Roberts University or any other entity...but by Oral Roberts, personally. Customarily, regardless of who holds the copyright, the author of a book is legally entitled to royalties from books he has written. However, if the author of a book which is given away or sold (by the millions) uses a non-profit religious organization in order to sell or give those books away, then the IRS gets interested. The IRS, in general, frowns upon a non-profit organization using *any* device which makes it possible for its officers to turn non-profit funds into personal fortunes.

For example, if the Oral Roberts Evangelistic Association pays to have books printed which Oral has written, then gives those books away to millions of people, and *then* turns around and directly pays Oral Roberts a royalty on the books, then he is directly converting non-profit funds into his personal pocket. The IRS doesn't like that and such activity can jeopardize an organization's non-profit status.

According to one of Oral's vice-presidents, the last book published which showed the copyright to be retained by Oral Roberts personally was *Miracle of Seed-Faith*. Over 1,225,000 copies of *Miracle of Seed-Faith* were printed in the timespan the book was given away on television, from January 1970 through February 1973. Actual figures on the royalties which Oral made on that book were not revealed to me, but it was indicated that the royalty scheme caused Oral some problems with the IRS...again, because of directly converting non-profit funds into personal revenue. In short, it appeared that Oral might not be able to continue receiving royalties from books marketed through ORA.

As a way of getting around IRS procedural regulations, a publishing "firm" was formed and the routing of funds allowed Oral Roberts and his family to continue receiving royalties on his books.

Pinoak Publications

Pinoak Publications was apparently "formed" sometime in 1974 and the first books which Oral Roberts wrote, showing Pinoak Publications as the copyright holder, appeared in 1975. Those books were *The Miracles of Christ* and *A Daily Guide to Miracles*. Between the two publications, nearly 2,000,000 volumes were printed and subsequently given away or sold.

The primary purpose of Pinoak Publications, as explained to me by Ron Smith, an ORU vice-president, was to allow Oral Roberts to continue receiving royalties from his books. Royalty revenues were used to establish a trust for Oral, Evelyn, and their children. Through Pinoak Publications, a direct conversion of nonprofit funds into a personal fortune was "avoided." In essence, royalties to Oral Roberts were not being paid directly to him by the Oral Roberts Association.

The Oral Roberts Association (ORA) would "purchase" the books from Pinoak Publications and then give them away to millions of Oral's television viewers. The vice-president mentioned above stated that ORA was paying Pinoak Publications $2.00 per book for every book printed.

The payoff

Pinoak Publications would then pay *actual* printing costs for the books...and the remaining monies were used to establish a family trust for Oral and his heirs. The actual printing cost for *A Daily Guide to Miracles,* however, could not possibly have been anywhere near $2.00 per book. There were at least eight printings of *A Daily Guide to Miracles* and the *smallest* printing run was for 100,000 copies. The other runs were for either 200,000 or 400,000 copies. When that many books are printed and bound at the same time, the actual printing costs have been estimated to be less than 50 cents per book. In other words, that left Pinoak Publications with something in the neighborhood of $1.50 per book to put into the family trust.

Between the two publications which show Pinoak Publications as publisher, nearly 2,000,000 volumes were printed. In very rough figures, that could amount to a personal slush fund...in the form of a family trust...in the neighborhood of $3,000,000. *And that's a pretty good neighborhood!*

Where is Pinoak Publications?

The inside cover of the two volumes mentioned states, "copyright 1975, Pinoak Publications, Tulsa, Oklahoma." From that, you would have reason to believe that such a firm actually existed in Tulsa. Pinoak Publications, however, has never been listed in the Tulsa telephone book. It has no address and my investigation turned up absolutely nothing which indicates that Pinoak Publications *ever really* existed as a business firm in Tulsa, Oklahoma. It was certainly not a corporation. No corporation by that name is listed with the Secretary of State in Oklahoma. Neither is Pinoak Publications listed as a proprietorship or limited partnership in either Tulsa or with the State Department of Oklahoma. In short, it never really existed as a *bonafide* publishing firm *anywhere!*

Why the secrecy?

Ron Smith, Executive Vice-President for ORU, revealed that Pinoak Publications was the most closely guarded secret within the organization. Why? Oral Roberts has received royalties from books in the past. The circumstances suggest that Oral Roberts, or his aides, established Pinoak Publications in order to give Oral one last personal stab at forming a personal and family trust that would set him up for life. One can only assume that the reasons for wishing to establish such a financial haven were based upon fears that perhaps someday, something bad would happen to Oral Roberts University. And, if something like that *were* to happen, Oral Roberts' personal financial picture could be jeopardized. Apparently, Pinoak was formed to ward off such a potential occurrence. And, certainly, a family trust fund with as much as $3,000,000 would keep the wolves away!

One can't help wondering, however, why there was so much secrecy surrounding Pinoak Publications. Was anything illegal done? I wouldn't tend to think so. Any illegal activity could jeopardize Oral's entire ministry and put a blight on the integrity of everything he had done up to 1975. Oral Roberts was, however, *extremely* sensitive about having Pinoak mentioned by anyone. He was so sensitive about the setup, in fact, that he *fired* one of his relatives because that individual began talking to ORA employees about Pinoak!

Ron Smith confided that the husband of one of Oral's daughters made some rather loose comments to personnel who worked in the Editorial Department of the Oral Roberts Association. The son-in-law's comments were paraphrased to me in this fashion: the son-in-law was purported to have said, "Look, you people need to think up some new ways to market more of Oral's books. The family wants more money to go into Pinoak!"

The ORA official who told me about the story was the person who had "squealed" on the young man. He had told Oral, "Look, Oral, you're going to have to talk with young (...). He's talking about Pinoak to other employees and you could end up having a problem because of it."

Well, Oral became incensed. Without allowing the ORU official to leave, Oral called his son-in-law into his office and fired him on the spot. He then called his daughter in and chewed *her* out also. The ORA official told me that he'd never seen anyone act so cold or callously toward their own flesh and blood in his life. He said, "Oral just absolutely cut both of them off, right there on the spot!" As he told me that, I was thinking, *what did you expect after you told Oral about it that way?*

At any rate, Oral's daughter and her husband weren't working on the campus of Oral Roberts University soon after that and, eventually, they both left town and are currently residing in Colorado. On two occasions, I did notice the daughter back in town and she once played the organ during a seminar. However, I never saw her husband on campus. *Once burnt, you don't return to the frying pan!*

Backing away from Pinoak Publications

Apparently, as a result of the "leak" relating to Pinoak Publications, the method of routing royalties to Oral Roberts was curtailed in 1976. For one thing, the first book to appear after the two Pinoak volumes was a publication entitled *Three Most Important Steps to Better Health and Miracle Living.* That publication was copyrighted in 1976 by the Oral Roberts Evangelistic Association. A later book, published in 1977, entitled *How to Get Through Your Struggles,* was also copyrighted by the Association.

It would appear that the Pinoak scheme was planned to have a short duration...that perhaps it was to go unnoticed by anyone and that, after a sizeable sum was accumulated for a family trust, future copyrights would be vested with the Oral Roberts Evangelistic Association.

In any event, questions or remarks about Pinoak Publications were always a hush-hush matter within the organization and remain that way today. Whatever type of "firm" it actually was remains a mystery. To reiterate, no record exists which reveals that it was ever an ordinary publishing firm. No address ever existed except *somewhere* in Tulsa, Oklahoma. It was never listed in a telephone book and efforts to trace its location, other than to identify the nominee administrator, have proven fruitless. It never really existed except on paper.

The facts remain: one man got fired for talking loosely about Pinoak and the man who fired him was his father-in-law, Oral Roberts himself. In addition, the actual costs of printing runs in the neighborhood of 200,000 copies per run *do not begin to approach $2.00 per book!* That sum, however, according to Ron Smith, is what Oral Roberts Evangelistic Association paid Pinoak. Informed persons in the printing business indicate that actual costs on such large printing runs would be much closer to something less than 50 cents per book. And while income tax returns apparently do exist for Pinoak Publications, those records are not available to the public. I doubt they ever will be.

But, in the event that some misfortune should fall upon Oral Roberts' ministry or the university which carries his name, he always has a very substantial family trust fund to tide him over in his golden years. And with the kind of money it looks as though was cleared through Pinoak, they should be golden years indeed!*

---

*Since first publication of the above, I've found at least one other book, *Christ in Every Book of the Bible*, to have come out with the Pinoak credit.

Chapter 9

Legitimizing a Windfall

What is a windfall?

Webster says a windfall is an unexpected legacy or gain. Most of us think in personal terms of a windfall as being something through which we might inherit a fortune from some unknown relative...where we suddenly come into lots of money unexpectedly. We've also heard accounts of someone who went into business, hit things just right, and struck a windfall through his endeavors. Gold miners, looking in vain for years for the illusive yellow nuggets, have suddenly struck a mother lode and hit a windfall. Some people have had their windfalls hit them on their heads without any effort on their part at all. Others have sought their windfall and found it.

Oral Roberts *sought* his windfall...from the earliest days of his ministry. Most of his own writings about the early days of his ministry reveal his frustrations with economics. In describing his early ministry, Oral has usually written about crowds that weren't big enough, large auditoriums that weren't available, or insufficient funds in order to either rent large auditoriums or buy his own tent. And, nearly always in his own accounts of his early ministry, he reveals a high level of frustration with his own economic situation. He didn't have enough money to pay his bills. Or, he didn't have enough money to buy the car he needed...*or wanted*.

And while he has always endeavored to project an image of being a person whose primary concerns were for other people's health, his life-style indicates a desire to get ahead that is expressed largely in economic terms. By his own account before he began his ministry, he ran away from home as a teenager to get away from poverty and religion. One can only wonder which aspect of his early life he disliked more...poverty or religion. Inasmuch as he went back into religion, one might conclude that he disliked poverty more.

The early days of Oral Roberts as a minister are somewhat revealing. He was hunting and pecking. *He was looking for something*. From his teenage days as an evangelist holding revival meetings, and then subsequently as the pastor of small churches in Toccoa, Georgia and Enid, Oklahoma, it is evident that Oral was looking for a way to "break through" in a way that would be big enough to satisfy his desires at that point in his life.

In his book *My Story*, Oral wrote, "When I left Toccoa for Oklahoma, I felt destiny had me by the hand and soon the *big* thing would happen to me...." In that same book, you find similar wording: "Destiny had carried me this far along, and I thank God for providentially arranging people and places and things to help me on my way." Notice that he wrote, *my way*, and wrote earlier of *big things* happening to him.

If you read enough of Oral's own writings, trace the development of his ministry, and look for the changes in his personal life-style as his ministry grew...such as the purchase of a 258-acre ranch near Tulsa dotted with expensive registered cattle and horses...you will inevitably have to conclude that financial success in his personal life was *very* important to Oral Roberts. The home on that ranch...and be reminded that this was in the mid-fifties...was appraised at $60,000. He also had a runway built onto the ranch to accommodate his 12-passenger executive plane. That relatively plush life-style is hard to equate with the comment he made to *Cosmopolitan* in 1956. "I am just God's humble instrument." *Humble, indeed.* At that same point in his life, some of Oral's employees were given the job of driving his children to Holland Hall, a private, expensive school in Tulsa, Oklahoma.

One has difficulties equating the connotations of "a humble servant" with such a life-style, that enjoyed among other things a total income reported at nearly $150,000 in 1955. At that point, however, he began to worry about his windfall being criticized. In *The Call,* Oral wrote, "I could not afford to allow people to equate healing prayers with money. I have often offended people because I refused the money they tried to put in my hand after I had prayed for them. I had promised God I would not touch the gold or the glory! I meant it." Perhaps he meant that he would not accept a direct, one-on-one gift from a pray*ee* to the pray*er,* but he *did* accept one "love" offering per week during his crusades and that amount alone reportedly totalled out to well over $30,000 per year...again during the fifties.

Oral Roberts knew it was going to happen that way, however. He knew he would eventually hit it big. As early as 1948, he began conducting his ministry in a businesslike manner and had it incorporated. In *The Call,* Oral wrote, "In July of 1948 I felt it best to incorporate into a nonprofit religious organization...absolute and final authority over all financial matters was put into the hands of a board of trustees. These were dedicated Christian businessmen who had not only an effective Christian witness but good business sense as well."

Oral's comment about entrusting absolute and final authority over financial matters to others is an outright falsehood. And it still is today. The Executive vice-president in charge of finance and endowment for the Oral Roberts Association revealed that he could not spend over $50,000 without Oral's approval. It would appear that perhaps Oral delegates absolute and final authority over financial matters as long as it doesn't involve spending over $50,000! Once you get into the "big coin," however, it requires his involvement. In addition, the actions and conversations of Oral Roberts' associates indicates that he doesn't hand over absolute and final authority to anyone over anything.

Characteristics of a religious windfall

The term "religious windfall" applies to any religious organization that takes on most of the following characteristics: 1) it survives as a nonprofit corporation; 2) it is headed by a self-appointed head or "personality"; 3) its delivery is through mass media such as television, radio, or magazines; 4) its programs are designed to appeal to people in ways that imply that the respondents should send in money to the organizations; 5) its funds are administered by trustees who have been carefully chosen by the head of the organization; 6) the organization carries the name of the founder; 7) the "programs" of the organization tend to aggrandize the capabilities of its founder; 8) there is an essence of "hero worship" inherent in the types of programs which the organization sponsors; 9) the programs of the organization appeal to people who want to get ahead financially, emotionally, or physically; 10) the authority of God is conveyed to have been transferred to the organization's founder or current head; 11) and, finally, the organization's head demonstrates an extraordinarily large ego.

If you're looking at any religious organization and thinking of contributing your own money to that organization, then you should check it out against the above characteristics. If your investigation results in a "yes" answer to many of the above characteristics, then you'd probably be better off spending your money somewhere else...perhaps with the local church of your choice, the United Way, or some other charitable organization that effects social improvements without enriching the pocketbook of the founder himself.

In an honest attempt to judge the Oral Roberts organization against such criteria, it is enlightening to analyze his ministry against each one individually. Such a critique follows below in the same order as listed above:

1) *The organization exists and survives as a nonprofit entity.* Oral Roberts had his ministry incorporated on a nonprofit basis in 1948. The incorporating officers were Oral Roberts, his wife Evelyn and Oral's brother, L. V. Roberts.

2) *The organization is headed by a self-appointed head or personality.* There can be no arguments about Oral Roberts being a TV personality. Also, he is all-powerful within his own organization. As previously stated, he once threatened to close ORU if the Dean of the School of Theology was not fired. Oral knew the Dean would get fired. The institution could not survive without him, Oral Roberts, and the faculty and administration of the university knew it.

3) *The delivery of the religious organization is through mass media.* The primary thrust of Oral's current-day ministry is through television. His program, "Oral Roberts and You" plays on 350 TV stations across the country and similar versions of programs are edited for radio to play on nearly 200 radio stations. His use of mass mailing techniques has resulted in the growth of a computerized mailing system that reaches out to 2.5 million homes.

4) *Programs encourage people to send money to the organization.* In August of 1962, *Life* magazine wrote of Oral's use of the *Blessing Pact,* a money scheme that guaranteed that if people gave $100 or more to his ministry, they'd get back the same amount or more from some other source within a year. The whole concept of Seed-Faith, along with the examples which Oral uses, serves to make people gullible when it comes to donating money to him.

5) *Funds are administered by trustees picked by the founder.* Inasmuch as Oral and Evelyn were co-founders of his nonprofit corporation, one can probably safely assume that any

trustees that he has picked see things his way. Oral seems always to have the final decision on who becomes a trustee on his board.

6) *The organization carries the name of its founder.* The name of Oral's "university" is Oral Roberts University. His television program is entitled, "Oral Roberts and You." His nonprofit corporation is named Oral Roberts Association. Both of these entities could have been given any name, but *his* name went on them.

7) *Organizational programs aggrandize the founder's capabilities.* One of Oral's books, *God's Formula for Success and Prosperity,* is replete with examples of people who did things according to *his* suggestions and then succeeded, mostly in financial ways. Nearly all of Oral's books have been filled with examples of people who were healed through attendance at one of Oral's crusades. Oral Roberts has *always* projected an image of being a faith healer who got results.

8) *Essence of "hero worship" directed toward organization's founder.* People who attend a seminar at Oral Roberts University look upon Oral as some kind of God. They ask him to autograph his books for them. They take pictures of him as he preaches. They send expensive gifts to him through the mail. Thousands of letters sent to him through the mails reveal that the writers look upon him as the driving force within their lives. Several of his TV specials have been deliberately designed (and, remember, I wrote some of these shows) to make it appear as if the television audience was awed by his presence. We deliberately formatted the shows so he could walk down through the crowd. He would encourage them on his way onto the set to reach up and touch him.

9) *Programs appeal to people who wish to succeed financially.* This gets at the very heart of the concept, Seed-Faith. The *emphasized* point of Seed-Faith, in its practical applications, is that if you give money to Oral Roberts or his organization, you will get a miracle back from God and be able to succeed yourself. It's sort of like a religious slot machine with a big sign over it reading, "Slug away and it

shall be slugged back unto you!" The more you give and the more you pull that charismatic handle, the better your chances are of finally striking it rich! If the concept of Seed-Faith were really as valid as Oral says it is, he would, in turn, be giving a lot of the money that comes in to some other organization...rather than spending it on buildings or programs that carry his name. I haven't seen Oral Roberts give *anything* away unless it served his purposes. I was once asked to wrangle a personal appearance for Oral Roberts on Jerry Lewis' MDA telethon. I called Jerry's producer and indicated that Oral Roberts would like to make a donation to MDA, but he wanted to deliver it personally to Jerry on his show. I was asked to make it clear that Oral didn't merely want to mail Jerry a check. He wanted to do it personally and appear on television with Jerry in front of millions of viewers who watch the telethon on Labor Day weekend.

10) *God's authority has been "transferred" to the organization's founder.* Oral Roberts uses this technique for everything it's worth. He *always* has. According to Oral, God told him to take His healing power to his generation. Over the years, Oral has repeatedly told the story about how God spoke to him. In one recent campaign designed to raise money for the City of Faith, Oral stated that God has spoken to him twenty-one times over the years. *Baloney!* If you were to go back over the years and compare the times God has "spoken" to Oral with the times he's needed money for some project, you'd probably find that God has somehow conveniently managed to make His conversations with Oral coincide with Oral's financial needs.

Personally, I'd absolutely *love* to be able to say that God spoke to me and told me to write this book about Oral Roberts...that God instructed me to reveal Oral as an exploiter of mass-marketing techniques in modern-day religion. But, I'm not going to lie to anyone about why this book is being written. The simple truth is this: I've grown up in the church; I've worked in or around religious or educational institutions much of my life; I have very deep feelings about what the church is and should be and after working for Oral Roberts for over three years as a writer who was instructed how to write for the man, I know that he is the smoothest fund-raiser who ever walked this earth. The flow of money is *always one way*...toward Oral Roberts' projects which bear *his* name and serve to separate him from the middle-class poverty which he hates so much.

11) *Organization's founder demonstrates extraordinary ego.* This characteristic is observable in the founders of nearly all ministries in the category of religious windfalls...and Oral Roberts is certainly no exception. There is evidence to indicate that he may, in fact, be out there in front setting the pace for the rest of the big-time preachers. Oral Roberts made it quite clear that his university would be named after him. Oral says that ORU is God's university. Why didn't Oral name it after God, then? Oral's television programs have his name in them..."Oral Roberts and You." Notice that *you* come in second! His parent corporation, initially named the Healing Waters Corporation, was changed to the Oral Roberts Evangelistic Association. Oral's ego is very much in evidence everywhere one looks on the Oral Roberts University campus.

Men with large egos tend to show off through their dress and the cars they drive. While Oral likes to tell how his mother told him to "stay humble, Oral," he is anything but humble. Oral's wardrobe is obtained from Brioni and most of the suits he wears each and every day have a price tag of at least $500. He wears $100 shoes and drives $25,000 cars which are replaced approximately every six months. He is a member of Southern Hills Country Club, the most prestigious and elite country club in Tulsa. The membership fee alone at Southern Hills Country Club is $18,000 (which includes a share of stock valued at $9,000) and, in addition to that, members are charged monthly dues of $130. Oral and his son also belong to the ultra-posh Thunderbird Country Club in Rancho Mirage,

California. They joined when a membership cost $20,000 each.

The jewelry which Oral has come to enjoy wearing on his hands and wrists has become a source of concern for some of his own employees in his Editorial Department...the department which puts out his monthly magazine. Artists within that department have begun putting an airbrush to his fingers and wrists in order to hide the diamond rings and the solid gold bracelets he has begun wearing within the past five years. I asked one employee why someone just doesn't ask Oral to take off his jewelry whenever he's having pictures taken and the employee replied, "No one has the nerve!"

At various places around the Oral Roberts "compound," one finds several parking places with Oral's name on them. He also has private drives which only he can use (through electronic gates) to get to the aerobics center, the Chapel, and of course his house. In Mabee Center, he has two private drive-in garages controlled by electronic openers which allow him to enter the building from two different points and avoid crowds which might tend to congregate around him.

All of those comparative luxuries would tend to point to the fact that Oral Roberts does have a rather large ego. In other words, Oral's employees, on their own initiative, don't merely build private drives with electronic gates up to certain buildings on campus. Oral asked for them.

Oral's office in the new addition of the Learning Resources Center, however, is the crowning glory to the demonstration of his ego. His office is larger than most homes. Certainly larger than most of the homes in which his partners dwell! In addition to a large reception area, his office is equipped with a plushly carpeted seating area that would make most people's living rooms look like tarpaper shacks by comparison. It is complete with a fireplace and a mantel which came from the Rothchild collection. The other furnishings are expensive, also.

133

The area which surrounds Oral Roberts desk, however, is what really demonstrates the ego the man carries with him. The area surrounding Oral's desk is larger than most living rooms. It is *raised* above the level, however, of the remaining expanses that make up his entire office. This raised area has a railing around it. When you walk into his office "on ground level," you are immediately forced into looking *up* at the man seated there behind a *huge* desk. It's not at all unlike walking into a courtroom and looking up at the judge's bench. One almost feels like uttering "Your Honor" before proceeding further into his office. The entire effect of his office has been architecturally designed to place Oral's desk and *him* above other persons in the room. No one with a normal ego would allow his architect to design and build such an office to work in. Estimates on the cost of Oral Roberts' office in the Learning Resources Center range as high as $100,000. And every bit of that money came from partners who sent in their donations for God's work at an average of about $10 per contribution. Using that average contribution of $10, one can only guess at who the lucky 10,000 partners are out there who helped Oral build the kind of office which he considers a suitable environment for doing God's work!

Safeguarding the secrets and the income

No religious organization can gain entry into the category of a windfall until it has begun to take in hundreds of thousands of dollars through its ministry. To be sure, the success of such ministerial windfalls depends mostly upon their capability to accumulate huge sums of money through the mails of Uncle Sam.

Oral Roberts has made comments to the effect that most ministries like to take their money in through the "front door." Oral believes that such practices are not subtle enough and he prefers to give things away (such as books and prayer cloths with his handprint upon them) through the "front door" and then rely upon the money to come in through the "back door." In other words, Oral looks upon giving millions of books away through the front door as a PR scheme that keeps him from looking like he's asking anyone for money. However, once you write in for the book, several subsequent mailings will subtly suggest that you should *then* give money (based upon the concepts of Seed-Faith which you'll read about in his books) to him and expect a miracle back. He considers this approach as getting money in through the back door.

And, like any back door operation, there are certain things the Oral Roberts Association would prefer to keep secret. For example, it is rather difficult to get into the Oral Roberts Association building without an appointment. Security guards are present to make sure that undesirables do not enter; and they check appointments with secretaries of executives who don't wish to be bothered by just anyone walking in off the street. Daily pickups of cash and checks are made by local Brinks trucks to take the money to the banks designated for such deposits.

The average reader would tend to downplay the significance of the dollar amounts spent through the "front door" in order for Oral Roberts to make his money through the back. The figures are, however, rather impressive. Oral Roberts television shows which play regularly on 350 television stations throughout the country fall into the category of "paid religion." Paid religion is a category of television shows that exists without a sponsor. Therefore, such shows sponsor themselves!

The costs are enormous. Oral Roberts spends well over $8 million per year just to buy television time! Through those television shows, he gives away as many as 500,000 books per year at a "cost" of $2.00 per book. That adds another $1 million per year to his television costs.

That investment through the front door of well over $9 million per year pays off, however. Oral Roberts receives annual donations through the mails and through seminars of nearly $60 million! From the way the figures speak for themselves, one can see that that leaves Oral with a lot of money: to put into pet projects like a university named after himself, fielding a publicity-generating basketball team...and into maintaining his lavish personal life-style.

Oral Roberts, however, is not the only evangelist in operation through the miracles of television and the electronic church. In addition to Oral Roberts, the Old Time Gospel Hour with Jerry Falwell spends a reported $14 million per year on radio and TV; the Christian Broadcasting Network spends $7 million; the PTL Network spends $8 million; Billy Graham spends $10 million; and Rex Humbard's Cathedral of Tomorrow program spends $8 million.

Those figures total up to $55 million per year being spent by religious "leaders" on television. They wouldn't be spending such sums unless the payoff was worth it and brought in much more than the monies spent! To illustrate, those same organizations bring in over $194 million per year in donations which result from them being on the air. That's nearly a four-to-one return on their investment and that's a good profit in any businessman's "rule book."

What good does it do?

One simple question seems to pop out of the mouths of people who learn how much money is spent each year on televised religion in this country: "What good does it do?" Well, there are the pet projects: Rex Humbard is building his grandiose Cathedral of Tomorrow. The Reverend Schuler is building an all-glass church. The Christian Broadcasting Network has its own satellite system. Billy Graham recently had to answer embarrassing questions about a $23 million trust fund administered in Texas, apparently originally earmarked for his brand of Christian university, which was never built. Certainly, wherever else the money goes, part of it assures comfortable living for the television ministers.

What good does all that money do? Does it help the people who have sent it in? *Only if they think it does!* And most of them do. But the way I see it, they're being played as suckers. A sucker is a bottom fish working the riverbed in search of some scrap of garbage that has floated down through the murky waters to its level. And many of the people who respond with money to television ministers feel themselves trapped at the bottom of life. They're desperately hopeful that some scrap of assistance will float down to them, that they'll be pulled up to prosperity, to love, to good health.

And television ministers give them everything they want: books, prayer cloths, annointing oil, special coins, special "key" clubs of prayer, plastic models of Jesus, or anything else that will make that sucker bite!

I don't mean to use the word "sucker" critically...although I know it sounds that way. People *are* vulnerable and gullible where their religion is concerned. Religion is, by its very nature, supernatural. Through religion, we answer the unanswerable questions in our lives. And when we turn to religion to meet some terrible need in our lives, we're all targets for the television ministers. If we have extraordinary needs, we tend to turn to something which might appear to have extraordinary powers. Inasmuch as we probably know the minister in our church as an ordinary person, we don't attribute extraordinary powers to him. On the other hand, the soft lights of television and the close-up shots that are used to enhance the visual impact of the television minister make us think that perhaps he does have something extraordinary with which to improve our lives. So, in our hour of need, we turn to the television minister rather than to the minister who serves us in our local church.

Does the television minister pray to a different, more power-ful God than our local minister? Is the television minister available seven days a week to help us or members of our family? Will the television minister come visit you in the hospital? Will the television minister be there with you, in person, to comfort you when you've lost a loved one? Can anyone but God comfort you over such a loss anyway?

This has been said previously in this book, but it deserves repetition: the minister in your local church deserves your admiration, your affection, your love, your respect, and the money out of your pocketbook much more than that television minister. You local minister isn't using the special effects of television, close-up shots, or costly Hollywood makeup men and hair stylists to make him look better to his church audience. He's merely there, working for God as a real human being and he's available to help you, *in person*. And, chances are, like all of the rest of us, he has some human faults of his own that he won't be able to hide through the marvels of television.

The next time you're tempted to give Oral Roberts *or any other television minister* a donation, just stop and think. Then double that amount and give it to the local minister or church of your choice. The more local the better. The closer to you the better. And, after you've done that, you still have the God-given right to expect back a miracle in your life...at the point of your need.

Give your local church a break. Give your local minister a chance. The only legitimate church in the world exists somewhere, on some street, *in your town*.

Chapter 10

Legitimate Windfalls and Personal Fortunes

In the previous chapter, it was demonstrated that the monies spent to put televised religion into your home are astronomical. Of equal importance, it was shown that the revenues back to such television ministries are even greater. One of the questions you might ask yourself is, "Where does that money go?"

Where does the money go?

Indirectly, because of the large sums of money which Oral's organizations deposit in Tulsa banks, he wields a great influence within the Tulsa business community. Other nationally known television ministers are just as guilty as Oral of using their fund-raising abilities to indulge themselves in personal monetary schemes. Rex Humbard once bought into a large girdle factory with some of the money he came by through religion. Do a bit of research into where and how television ministers live, and you'll see where a substantial amount of offerings go.

Most of the big television evangelists have their own executive planes, drive big cars, have large expensive homes where they can "spend time with God" and have personal wardrobes that would make the average movie star's mouth water.

Their private lives tend to be secluded from the general population through use of security systems that surround their estates; and some of them change their unlisted telephone numbers routinely.

Oral Roberts' personal estate, *La Casa La Paz,* is surrounded by a large security fence built of metal and wood. Special electronic devices (sound sensors and motion detectors) are required to open the gates onto his estate and a security house is on the grounds with 24 television cameras which let Oral's three security guards know if anyone has climbed over his fence.

In addition to the money which is spent on private luxuries, there are other ways in which nationally known ministers spend their money to increase their sphere of influence within their own state or community.

Control and influence

Money talks. It always has and it always will. And the big-time evangelists reveal a remarkable dexterity in making their money talk for them. If used properly, an evangelist with a cash flow of several million dollars through his organization can eventually be perceived as a positive force by businessmen in his own community. And while the businessmen within the community may not agree with an evangelist's brand of religion or agree with his methods in exploiting it, they do tend to agree that it's good to have his money in *their* community rather than somewhere else.

Banking Oklahoma-style: parlez vous greenbacks?

Bankers tend to be very nice to big-time evangelists: they want part of that multi-million dollar cash flow going through their bank. And the shrewd evangelist will make use of that desire and spread his money around in several banks. If done properly, the evangelist (or his relatives, or friends, or close associates) will ultimately be asked to become a director on a bank board that enjoys a large cash flow from the evangelist's organization. Oral once asked that his wife, Evelyn, be placed on the board of the First National Bank of Tulsa and when they refused, he withdrew much of the money he had on deposit there.

Under optimum conditions, and with good planning, an evangelist such as Oral Roberts can eventually end up, either personally or through proxy representation, on the boards of several banks.

For example, Oral's Vice-President for Finance and Endowment once served concurrently as a director on the boards of the following banks: First National of Oklahoma City; Bank of Commerce in Tulsa; First National of Miami, Oklahoma; the Grove Bank of Grove, Oklahoma; and the Delaware County Bank in Jay, Oklahoma. Oral Roberts, himself, is a member of the board of directors for the Bank of Oklahoma in Tulsa.

How it got started

As indicated above, Oral trusts only relatives or close associates to represent his money. Occasionally, he trusts an attorney or two who has been associated with him for a number of years. Who he uses depends upon the situation.

When Oral Roberts' son-in-law (Marshall Nash) died, his probate listed him as owner, partner or investor in the following enterprises: Barton Insurance Agency of Tulsa; Tri-State Insurance of Prague, Oklahoma; M. E. Nash, Inc.; Bank of Commerce in Tulsa, Oklahoma; First National of Miami, Oklahoma; First National Bank of Prague, Oklahoma; the Bank of Grove, Oklahoma; Bank of the Lakes, Langley, Oklahoma; American Bank of Tulsa; 1st Tulsa Bancorporation; Nash and Mobley, Incorporated of Tulsa; Port

Properties of Tulsa; Riverside Investments, Inc. of Tulsa; and the Kensington Company of Tulsa.

The Barton Insurance Agency was used for some time almost exclusively by the Oral Roberts Association to insure its properties. One of its employees actually officed in the insurance department of the Oral Roberts Association. At about the time Marshall Nash died, one ORA insurance department employee moved into the Barton Agency to assume further administrative duties.

The original Bank of Commerce stock which Marshall Nash bought was reportedly purchased through a loan which was guaranteed by the Oral Roberts Association. One can only wonder whether the IRS considers it proper for a nonprofit religious corporation to secure or guarantee a loan to the son-in-law of the organization's founder. Lately, Oral Roberts sold his 37% interest in this bank.

Prior to the probating of Marshall Nash's will, one of Oral's VP's began sitting in on board meetings and was eventually named as a director of three of the banks which Marshall Nash had owned stock in. This was no surprise since in Marshall Nash's will, much of the stock and holdings which he had been able to amass during his years as a Tulsa business-man were given back to the Oral Roberts Association. Marshall Nash, while credited with being an astute business-man, could not possibly have built up the fortune he acquired had he not had the backing of Oral's organization. And when he died, a stock portfolio worth millions of dollars was left to the Oral Roberts Association. His children inherited trust funds that were much less substantial.

Riverside Investments, Inc., another of Nash's enterprises, was reportedly the purchaser of Turkey Mountain which lies across the Arkansas River in the path of 71st Street. Marshall's brother, Bill Nash, is now chairman of the Transportation Committee for the Oklahoma Department of Transportation and there has been heavy emphasis on getting a bridge built across the Arkansas which would connect 71st Street and the

Okmulgee Beeline...through Turkey Mountain, of course. Such a bridge would greatly increase the present value of Turkey Mountain and add considerably to the bulk of family-controlled properties.

Kensington Properties is the developer for the apartment housing and shopping center which is across from Oral Roberts University and United Bank...of which Marshall Nash and then Bill Nash have been president. Other partners in Kensington, in addition to Marshall Nash, are John Williams, Sr., John Williams, Jr., Burl McIntosh, Jack Santee (attorney for the Oral Roberts Association), a Tulsa oilman named Rabinowitz, and Stuart Golding of Tampa, Florida.

Marshall Nash was a fair businessman and a good family man. His wife Rebecca, who was Oral's oldest daughter, was a fine woman and loving mother. I was impressed by her dignity, her integrity, and her down-to-earth charm. Occasionally, she would write an article for "Abundant Life" and her approach to Christianity was straight-forward and simple. She did write her own articles, rather than having a ghost writer do it for her, like Oral does.

Nonetheless, as fine a couple as Marshall and Rebecca Nash were, there can be no doubt that the $10 million estate they accumulated during their marriage was derived from benefits they enjoyed through Oral's influence in the Tulsa business community. There are ways to increase personal wealth and expand spheres of influence without breaking laws. Bank presidents are human and the profits which their banks turn over result in large part from the types of deposits which their banks are able to attract. If the founder of an organization (which deposits several million dollars per year in a bank) implies that he'd appreciate it if that bank would favorably review a loan application from the founder's son-in-law, that bank president will, if he's smart, make sure that such a loan is approved.

Inasmuch as money and influence tend to beget more money and more influence, it should be no real surprise to anyone that Marshall Nash did, indeed, succeed in his business ventures. There is nothing really wrong with any of that, if you understand and agree with the free enterprise system. The sons or close relatives of wealthy men do tend to expand family wealth, if they have any brains at all. And Marshall Nash did have his share of brain-power.

There would seem to be some serious questions raised, however, by the knowledge that a nonprofit *religious* organization is able to use money and power, the traditional tools of the hard-driving businessman, to expand the personal fortunes of those who have *family* ties with the organization's founder. Again, no laws broken...but great personal fortunes amassed in a comparatively short period of time. Traditionally, we tend to think of religious organizations as collectors of money which then distribute such funds toward those with needs in the community. Most churches tend to have such programs. The entire thrust of the Salvation Army, for example, is to collect goods, money, etc., from those who have it and then give it away to those with need.

Oral Roberts' organization, however, is characterized by a pattern of collecting and using money in ways which personally enrich the pocketbooks of family members. For example, when University Village (Oral's retirement center) was built, the construction firm which got the job was Marshall Nash's own firm. The former president and administrator of University Village (now a vice-president of Oral Roberts University and Association) once jokingly informed me when I was in Florida that the Oral Roberts Association was paying out millions of dollars to have University Village built by a contractor who was a family member. Profits off that job went directly back into the family coffers.

Again, no laws broken. While nepotism laws govern the conduct of public officials who work for federal and state institutions, those laws do not apply to religious nonprofit organizations. If the founder of such an organization wishes to use nonprofit funds and have his son-in-law build a multi-million dollar complex with those funds, then there is nothing illegal about letting that son-in-law make a profit. *But, it does result in nonprofit funds being converted into personal fortunes.*

There are other ways of becoming wealthy simply by working for such an organization. If, by luck or circumstances, an employee of Oral's becomes privy to certain procedures and plays the game, he will eventually be rewarded in one way or another. The former administrator of University Village, for example, is now Oral Roberts' Chief of Staff. When he went to work for Oral, he was on a salary of $12,000 per year. Shortly after the construction project at University Village, that administrator was made a vice-president. He was *given* a home to live in. He was *given* a Buick Riviera car to drive. Today that individual owns TTG, the Hollywood recording studio in which Oral Roberts' World Action Singers and orchestras did their recordings for years. He drives a $33,000 Mercedes sports car. He owns stock in a building that Marshall Nash formerly had an interest in. He became a director on bank boards which Marshall Nash had owned stock in.

When I left Oral Roberts organization, I was offered an income for life...apparently just to keep my mouth shut about the organization. I turned down the offer and I would have kept my mouth shut anyway if Oral Roberts hadn't disgusted me with the way he went about his City of Faith project. More about that in another chapter about the City of Faith.

What should be done to stop religious ripoffs?

Stringent laws should be passed which would make it absolutely impossible for the founder of a nonprofit religious organization to reap a personal fortune. There should be no way the founder, his family, or any of his associates would be able to convert millions of nonprofit dollars into personal fortunes. Construction bids related to religious organizations should go through the same processes required by state and federal organizations.

No family member should be able to obtain "sweetheart" loans that are backed formally or informally by the nonprofit corporation.

Founders and executives of religious nonprofit corporations should not be allowed to serve as directors on bank boards or as executives on underwriting insurance agencies.

Complete and open reporting on tax returns should be required of all religious nonprofit corporations. Public disclosure should also be required of the founder, his family, and his executives.

The use of nominee accounts through banks, law firms, and accounting firms should be made unlawful when utilized by a religious nonprofit corporation.

Executives of religious nonprofit organizations should not be allowed to buy or own businesses which the firm does business with.

The founder or chief personality of a religious organization should not be allowed to receive personal royalties from books he has written which will be marketed through his religious nonprofit organization. Inasmuch as the author's story when he writes such a book is "that God laid this on my heart" or "God told me to write this book," the financial rewards from authoring such a book should go entirely back into doing more of God's work...rather than lining the author's wallet! When a man who has written a recent book is talking into a television camera before 50 million viewers one can wonder whether his enthusiasm over the book is hinged on potential profits for himself or actual beliefs that the book will do wonders for its readers.

The entire structure of nonprofit religious corporations should be reviewed by the IRS and other government agencies. It is no mere accident that the Reverend Jones, the Reverend Moon, and others have accumulated huge fortunes through the use of current laws regulating religious nonprofit entities. While the several religious denominations we are familiar with are certainly legitimate organizations that do a great deal of good, it is questionable whether the federal government should be guilty of having passed laws that allow non-denominational ministers to establish huge followings and huge personal fortunes...under the guise of religion.

It is one thing to safeguard the works of both national and local denominational, and independent churches through nonprofit status. It is quite another matter, however, when current laws allow nearly anyone with a definable religious belief to get his wheel of fortune turning out millions of dollars per year!

Religious ripoffs, the FCC and the postal service

Recently, an official of the Armstrong religious conglomerate in California compared his organization to a government...with all of its rights and privileges. That's a bunch of baloney and ought to be viewed accordingly. To be sure, certain aspects of nationwide ministries are similar in nature to the federal government. As a case in point, the federal government collects taxes from citizens in all the 50 states. Similarly, nationwide ministries collect contributions from citizens all over the country. The similarity stops there, however. The federal government redistributes millions of tax dollars through revenue sharing and all the states benefit through that procedure. And there are certain efficiencies which result through having federal taxes collected once each year and then having those funds redistributed back to the 50 states on a per capita basis.

"Personality" ministries seldom do that, however. They collect monies from all over the country *and then they keep the money primarily in their own communities.* Funds or benefits from such funds rarely if ever find their way back into the several communities around the country. The result is that

147

thousands of good churches around the country are losing funds which they need...and they're losing them to fat and wealthy ministries such as Oral Roberts', the Reverend Moon's, the Reverend Ike's, the Reverend Jones', etc.

The manner in which nationwide ministries build such windfalls is primarily through television, radio, and the mails. And the effect is not unlike a cancer that gets spread all over the country. These "big money" ministries are proliferating because of the gullibility of the public. The Bible predicted that there would be false teachers who, "through covetousness shall...with feigned words make merchandise of you" (2nd Peter 2:3) and will "with good words and fair speeches deceive the hearts of the simple (innocent)" (Romans 16:18). Christians are warned to "mark" or identify such men and withdraw from all ministries that "suppose that gain is Godliness" (1 Timothy 6:3-6). That particular scripture turns Oral's concept of *Seed-Faith* into a sham!

I would recommend that *all* religious organizations, because of their tax-exempt status, be made accountable to the public...that their financial affairs be made just as public as a bank's. I would further recommend that guidelines be established by both the FCC and the postal department...the effects of which would be to enforce fair and honest practices when soliciting money through religious organizations.

There is also a matter to be considered which is very closely related to the position the FCC has taken with regard to honesty in advertising. Ministries which use questionable tactics...such as offering prayer cloths, annointing oil and other gimmicks that are designed just to raise money...should be forbidden to continue. This would force all ministries to raise money *only* on the merits of their service to the public.

Summarily, all religious organizations should be required to publish a financial statement once a year and be required to mail it to *everyone* who has donated money to that organization over the year. Full and complete disclosure of all income, expenditures, investments, income from investments, cash on hand, and all other holdings should be required material in such an annual report to the constituents of such religious organizations. The honest religious organizations won't mind doing this at all. In fact, many of them are asking that such procedures be required. Further, many religious organizations are doing it now *on their own,* in spite of the fact that it isn't required!

Quite obviously, there are many churches and religious organizations doing a good job of presenting their religious beliefs to the public and making legitimate appeals for funds. In addition, certain "para-church" organizations such as the Salvation Army, World Vision, Campus Crusade, The Navigators and Young Life have a good record of proving fiscal responsibility to the public. From my observations, the organizations which have nothing to hide (or be embarrassed about) have shown their willingness to reveal their full financial situation. In contrast, the Oral Roberts Evangelistic Association has, in the past, refused to provide financial statements to both the Tulsa Chamber of Commerce and the Better Business Bureau.

Recent publications, including the *Wall Street Journal,* have run articles which revealed that certain large television ministries have actually misallocated, misappropriated, or misused funds which were donated for specific purposes. The funds were actually used for purposes other than those for which they were donated. Under certain circumstances, such practices can be construed to be illegal and, indeed, fines and penalties have been imposed upon such organizations which have been guilty of such mismanagement.

In summary, there is absolutely no reason why a *religious* nonprofit organization should want to withhold information about its finances...unless, of course, something embarrassing, unethical or illegal has been done with donated funds. If the sheer volume of donations is embarrassing to a religious organization, then let the organization *be* embarrassed about it! A retired widow on social security who is considering pledging $50 a month to a religious organization has the right to know that it already has $100 million in donations on hand and can do quite nicely without any sacrifice on her part!

Chapter 11

Hypocrisy
in the Hierarchy

During my professional life on college campuses, I never witnessed any organization so rife with hypocrisy as Oral Roberts University or the Oral Roberts Evangelistic Association. To the public, Oral Roberts' message is clear: his people don't drink, smoke, swear, have marital problems, or show any greed when it comes to the acquisition of material wealth. According to Oral Roberts, ORU is a bastion of academic freedom governed by Christian principles, filled with faculty and students whose daily lives are guided by Christ. Peaceful harmony would appear to prevail within every nook and cranny of his organizations.

In reality, however, there are plenty of examples which lead one to conclude that Oral Roberts' organizations place more emphasis on show than substance, pay more homage to wealth than wisdom, and dance to the tune "Oh, Lord, Won't You Buy Me a Mercedes Benz!"

Drinking in private or out of town

The unwritten code which seems to be practiced by many ORU and ORA officials is simply *don't get caught!* In other ds, you don't really have to be a Christian, you just need to be sneaky. I have seen some ORU officials drink in the privacy of their homes, and others have imbibed freely when they were out of town on institutional business. It is worthy to note that for many people, a social drink is not against their "laws." Those people really won't understand why I call it hypocrisy when Oral's employees drink. But, for those readers who are familiar with the Pentecostal movement, and all of its "do nots," the practice of drinking will be understood as a sin.

One ORU Vice-President keeps his beer in a refrigerator in his garage. The refrigerator inside the house might be peeked into by visiting ladies during faculty teas, or other social occasions, so beer isn't kept there.

Several high-ranking ORU officials seem to have a love for riding motorcycles, and those individuals often take their beer with them on their motorcycles, packed away inside the "tote bags" on the back of their bikes. They'll ride for miles to get out of Tulsa, park their bikes, for example, along the shores of Lake Okmulgee, and break out their beer.

I went for a motorcycle ride with an ORU official and two World Action Singers one Saturday afternoon in 1975 and we all ended up with our swimming suits on, with six-packs opened for some good, clean Christian fun...swimming in the lake and sipping suds. At that point, I was still trying to figure the place out and I didn't know if those people were really going to drink that beer or just find out if I would take a drink. Well, we all sat around that lake after taking a short dip, drank our beer, and talked about upcoming television shows for Oral Roberts. On another occasion which involved riding motorcycles, we finished taping a segment for "Oral Roberts Is Love," roared out for a high-speed ride down the Beeline to Sapulpa, and stopped in a Pizza Hut and sat there downing pizza and draft beer.

On another occasion, prior to a production meeting for the taping of "Oral Roberts at Grandfather Mountain," I smelled beer on the breath of a close associate of Oral Roberts. I told him I could smell the beer on his breath and, as Richard Roberts walked into the room with Patti, the man whirled and left the room to buy some Clorets. That man *knew* he wasn't supposed to have the smell of beer on his breath. That same man later led our production group in prayer, after our business meeting had been concluded!

My barber has a salon near ORU. He has also cut the hair of Oral Roberts and Richard Roberts. My barber knows I used to work for Oral Roberts and generally, when I'm in his shop, our conversation eventually touches upon Oral's organization. In March of 1979, when I was having my hair cut, this barber asked me if I knew that Richard Roberts drank. I hesitated for a moment and then replied that I'd heard such rumors, but that I didn't think there was any substance to them. Parenthetically, I should say that my barber has an Afro hairstyle. To continue, my barber mentioned that Richard had called him and made an appointment to go in for a trim. As they talked, Richard asked the barber if he liked his hair done in an Afro. The barber replied that it was easy to care for, that all it required was regular shampooing, and drying...that very little combing was necessary. Richard replied that he would like to have one but that his Dad wouldn't let him wear it that way. Richard Roberts is thirty-years-old! He should be able to wear his hair any way he wants.

After the barber had finished Richard's hair...apparently this was late in the day...Richard asked him if he'd like to come up to his house for a drink. Richard mentioned that his wife, Patti, was out of town and that he was all alone.

The barber went and had a drink with Richard. He told me that Richard had a full bar in his home...stocked with all the necessary liquors to fix just about any kind of drink anyone would want! And the barber had no reason to lie about the above circumstances. For one thing, people who do personal work for the Roberts' family tend to be rather well-paid and if the barber wanted the business they gave him, he would have had plenty of reasons not to mention the occasion at all.

I then asked the barber if he liked working on Oral's hair. He replied that he didn't enjoy working around Oral at all. The barber said that Oral had made fun of him, had asked him why he was so short; and then the barber concluded, "I think Oral likes to put people down!" I've heard Oral "put people down" and many people who've worked around him have felt the brunt of his temperament.

Smoking in private and out of town

It took me quite some time to realize what a "vanilla stick" is. I heard the term quite a few times in the Oral Roberts Association building, but sort of passed it off as some kind of term that perhaps was known only to those who were charismatic. One day an ORA employee came into my office and asked me if I'd like to take a break and go get a "vanilla stick." I asked, "What in the world is a vanilla stick?" The man replied in a whisper, "A cigarette!" I thought to myself, *this is probably a trick*. So I asked the man, "You smoke?" He replied, "Oh, yeah." I then asked him, "Isn't that against the rules?" He answered, "Yes, but as long as you're careful and don't let anyone see you, I guess it doesn't really matter that much."

I should reveal that I presently smoke about a half-pack of Carlton's a day. When I went to work for Oral Roberts, the man who hired me told me that I couldn't smoke on campus, and that I shouldn't smoke during the day. However, if I went away from campus for lunch, and there weren't any ORU employees around, I could discreetly have a cigarette. He then suggested that I chew gum on the way back to campus to take the smell of tobacco off my breath. I decided that I should probably quit smoking and did...down to the point where I was only having a few cigarettes a week after evening meals...but when I found out what "vanilla stick" meant and realized how many people within the organization used the term, I decided to forget going through the rigors of quitting cigarettes.

Marital problems in private or out of town

If you'll give Oral Roberts your best...that is, your biggest bill...you'll probably never have any marital problems. Somewhere along the line, Richard and Patti must have forgotten to kick in their donation!

In spite of Oral's efforts to convince everyone otherwise, many of his employees are actually normal people. They have good days and bad days and some of them don't get along with their spouses very well. Divorce, within Oral's organization, is considered to be one of those things that can get you put on the list of "suspects." If, after your divorce, you show signs of living a normal life and don't develop any of the symptoms of a Hell-bent-for-leather-sinner, you can get over the stigma of a divorce and continue to work effectively for Oral Roberts.

Interestingly enough, though, if you eventually meet someone you'd like to marry...after having been divorced once...you have to go through a rather special procedure. Divorced faculty members at ORU who wish to remarry must petition the Board of Regents and receive permission to remarry...if their former spouse is still living. Biblically speaking, a divorced person cannot remarry while the first spouse is still living...without committing adultery. That's to be found in the Chapter of Luke, you can look it up for yourself.

Oral Roberts has his own interpretation. If the Board of Regents agrees, you can remarry...even though your former spouse is still living...and apparently not be guilty of adultery. While I am admittedly not an expert on the epistemological merits of marital doctrines, this entire procedure seems asinine. Either the Bible is true *and to be followed*...or it isn't. I can only surmise that in one of God's conversations with Oral (one of those 21 times that Oral has mentioned), God gave

Oral permission to have his Board of Regents review each divorce and petition for remarriage and then make a decision based on the circumstances.

Divorce appears to be one of the painful realities we live with in today's world and there seems to be little doubt that some people can lead much better lives once they're divorced. What I have never understood, however, is why *anyone*, including Richard and Patti, should ever be forced to petition some board of *men* for permission to remarry.

If divorce is accepted in modern society, then remarriage must also be accepted. Again using the Bible as a reference, the only acceptable religious grounds for divorce is adultery. The word "incompatibility" is not found anywhere in the Bible. Apparently, however, incompatibility *is* acceptable grounds for divorce. And if that's all it takes to get you out of a marriage, then any further authority by man over remarriage has to be rejected on very simple and logical terms.

Hypocritical Christianity

All of us make mistakes in our lives for which we're often sorry. As the saying goes, "To err is human." Many people compensate for the wrong they do by participating in some kind of religious tradition such as Passover, Lent, confessions, etc. In any event, most of us try our best to do what is right; we live with and accept our human faults, and attempt to maximize the good we see in ourselves. Still, we often fall short of our goals because we are not "men of God."

There is a point, however, when a human (who represents himself as an appointee of God) should no longer exhibit so many of the faults that the rest of us live with in our own lives. One finds it difficult, for example, to imagine Billy Graham totally losing his temper and throwing a tantrum because of something that went wrong. A man of God simply is not supposed to act that way. And, to my knowledge, Billy Graham *does not* act that way.

Oral Roberts does, however, and so do many of his top associates. Losing one's temper is almost a way of life for Oral Roberts and those who work around him. When Oral Roberts was initially turned down on his application for a Certificate of Need for the City of Faith, he stormed out of the room, obviously angry and obviously unconcerned about letting anyone see his anger. His walkout was shown on local television stations in Oklahoma and it wasn't the anger of a man filled with some sort of righteous indignation based upon higher authority. It was more like a pout—childish and adolescent. If Oral Roberts had stuck out his lower lip and stamped his foot on the floor and screamed, "I want my Certificate of Need," he couldn't have been any more obviously un-Christian.

Oral Roberts on television is convincingly seen as a genuinely warm human being who understands people's problems and cares about them. He has even cried on television, or had tears come into his eyes at particularly appropriate moments in his sermons or prayers. *It is largely an act.* I've had occasion to coach him on his timing.

I've been backstage during productions and helped coach him into presenting an idea or a concept convincingly. Most of the time, however, it was my job to talk with Oral's producer and tell *him* what he needed to get Oral to do on camera in order for it to be "right." Because of my own church background, and my experience with various forms of public persuasion, I qualify as something of an expert when it comes to knowing what is *effective* in religious programming.

There is such a thing as having valid emotional religious experiences...and such religious emotions are not at all unlike other emotions we feel when we are moved by *something* in our lives...such as the birth of our own child, or the death of someone we have loved very much. Those emotions are real. But, they can also be portrayed. The memorable films we've seen, for example, which seem to win the awards at the end of the year are generally films which have contained powerful acting by men and women who convincingly portrayed what we recognized as "real" human trauma and emotions. It was the realistic representation of human life that *made* those films.

Occasionally, we'll read about an actor or actress who has starred in a powerful film and learn of some petty, vicious comment they've made. Or we'll read about something in their personal lives that seems extremely uncharacteristic of them in light of the powerful roles we've seen them play in films.

When we read of such things, it is generally a mild shock because we have forgotten that the actor is, after all, *an actor*. What we saw in the film was a portrayal of the characteristics of an admirable human being. The person who had the capability of portraying those characteristics, however, may not in real life be all that admirable.

Oral Roberts *is* such a man...and I base that statement upon my experiences in working with him along with comments made to me by persons who have worked for him much longer than I did. I can't think of anyone I know, other than Oral Roberts, whose wife has hidden his car keys in order to keep him from going out and driving a high-powered car down the road in a blind rage. A woman who does that for her husband is afraid of what that man might do to himself or someone else. And the perspective of such a man *cannot be Christian* when his actions cause his wife to do such a thing.

Oral Roberts is an accomplished actor who ought to get an Emmy for his portrayal of a caring human being. In reality, during a normal work week that doesn't involve being in front of a camera, he is often a hard-driving unsympathetic individual who steps on people. And the enjoyment he seems to feel in that kind of behavior probably comes from his own insecurities. It has been my experience that people who are happy with themselves do not strike out at others who are defenseless. A man, for example, who will make one of his employees cringe, "eat crow," and accept humiliation in front of others because he needs his job, is not the type of person we would rate very high. And that kind of person certainly does not deserve to be classified as a Christian leader. I could recount several instances in which I observed Oral Roberts humiliate people around him. But, the only reason I won't is that it would only serve to further humiliate those persons who have already felt the brunt of Oral's irascible temper. It is sufficient to say that the people who work around him the most are the ones who get "burnt" the most. Futher, I'm convinced that those who work around him closely...and stay on...have a certain masochistic strain in their own personalities. They'd have to enjoy it, at least subconsciously, or they wouldn't stay.

There is another aspect of Oral's un-Christian personality that has always intrigued me: and that is his utter disdain and contempt for other preachers whose ministries are not on a large scale like his. He has often made contemptuous comments which degrade the role of the traditional pastor. For example, "He's just a small-time preacher"; "You sound like just another preacher" or "I don't want to say that. I sound like a preacher talking!" To further illustrate Oral's attitude, those of you who saw Oral on the "Tomorrow" show with Tom Snyder will remember that Oral called Tom Snyder "just a frustrated preacher."

In retrospect, it is obvious that Oral Roberts does not respect the role of the traditional pastor. And I view that aspect of his nature to be utterly contemptible. I also see it as a revealing insight into Oral Roberts' character. Does Oral actually possess any innate desire to be a "man of God"? Or does he really desire prestige, wealth, power, and influence? Everything I see about the man—his habits, his projects, his sense of self-image, and his life-style—leads me to feel there is no other conclusion than that his ambitions and behavior are fundamentally "worldly," his priorities other than those of a man of God. I think both what I have revealed in the preceding pages and the examples that follow substantiate my conclusion.

Oral Roberts, when in front of an audience, is amazingly convincing at projecting an image of being humble. He rather enjoys putting on the "face" of humility and his reason for enjoying it is very simple: he loves to act. His projected humility, however, is a facade...for, in fact, he is one of the most egotistical men to ever breathe free air. A humble man does not keep dogging one of his top executives until the man finally wises up and hangs one picture...that of Oral Roberts...in the Founder's Room. A humble man does not have an office built for him (on the top floor of one of his buildings) and have the office designed in such a manner that anyone coming into the area has to "look up" at the man seated behind the desk. A humble man does not personally oversee the construction and decoration of space that is going to be used by him and make sure that every available comfort is included in such space.

A humble man does not pay his basketball coach $250,000 per year when there is no substantive reason why that quarter of a million dollars should not be given to the poor and needy Christians in this country who could use a "leg up." But is Oral Roberts really interested in helping the poor and needy? True, he will allow them to go through a healing line, but I see that as an ironic gesture of self-aggrandizement—he wants their admiration. But what does he do of a solid nature to really help them? He would rather spend $2.5 million over a ten-year period on a basketball coach...and, again what in the name of Heaven does a winning basketball team have to do with administering a "Christian" university. Example after example can be produced to make the point that when Oral spends money a primary consideration in spending it is for *show*. I find Oral Roberts to be an incorrigible showoff!

Oral Roberts loves to make a point of the relatively modest salary that is paid to him by Oral Roberts University. To be sure, $29,500 per year is a relatively modest amount...and like he says, he does pay some of his staff members more than that. *However*, there is a point that can be reached where a reported salary is not actually of any importance at all. Oral Roberts has stated on television that his television wardrobe is separate from his personal wardrobe...implying that he does not wear Brioni suits when he's functioning in the Learning Resources Center of ORU as its president. That is a bald-faced lie. I managed the television production department for ORU and know *exactly* where all television wardrobe clothing was kept and stored. Oral *never* kept one suit there in the three years I helped produce his television shows. What *is* true is that the Oral Roberts Association buys his clothes, justifies it because of him being on television, and he then wears those clothes while functioning in roles other than on television... when he's acting out the part of "man of God." He tends to downplay the significance of the big cars he drives by informing critics that those cars are given to him to drive. It really doesn't matter whether those cars are given to him. If they weren't given he'd buy them! Nonetheless, if *you* want to go out and buy a Mercedes, it is going to cost you about $25,000. If you *have* the money to buy the car, but don't need to because someone *gives* you the car to drive, it's the same as having kept that $25,000 right there in your pocket. But, what matters is not *how* Oral happens to drive big, expensive cars. The point *is,* he *does* drive them and will continue to do so...one way or the other! You'll never see Oral Roberts driving around in a Pinto or a Chevette...unless one of his top aides persuades him to do so after having read this particular chapter!

Hypocrisy in the healing line

I haven't seen that Oral Roberts prays for anyone's healing unless there's something in it for him. While he denies this and says that he doesn't pray for people for money, the facts speak differently. In his "seminars," he prays for people after they have collectively pledged an amount that generally ranges from $1.5 million to $3 million. It is revealing to note that the pledge service comes first...then the healing line. I have seen people who come to the campus seeking only Oral's prayers turned away in droves.

Nearly every day of the week, hundreds of people visiting the campus eventually end up in the Prayer Tower. The ones who are looking for Oral are told that he isn't available, that he is out of town, that he is busy, or that he is involved in some activity that will keep him from being able to pray for the sick that day. People who are persistent are then told where he lives. Many of them then walk up the hill and find a huge security fence with a gate that won't open unless you have the right electronic opener. At the gate, the guard then turns the people away and they leave Tulsa disenchanted and, of course, still ill and un-prayed for. In rare instances, where important people are involved or when it is quite apparent that there simply is no graceful way out of it, Oral does occasionally pray for someone. But, those are rare occasions, indeed. Most often, Oral's personal assistant turns such people away or directs them to someone else on campus who might have the time or the inclination to pray for them. I have been asked several times during or after tapings to "keep those people away from Oral."

I submit that a "man of God" who had been told by God to take His healing power to Oral's generation would not turn people away who came to him for prayers. It seems very revealing, indeed, that with *very* few exceptions, Oral only prays for people when there is a fund-raising scheme built into the program. The fact that he prays for peoples' healing on television does not water down my point, at all. The television prayers are used to attract sick and hurting people to his television shows, to get them to write in for one of his books about healing or becoming financially successful, which then allows his direct mail experts to begin sending those people mail which does ask for money.

Oral Roberts has never said that God told him to pray for the sick when he had time or just when he was raising money. According to Oral, God merely told him to take His healing power to Oral's generation. It would seem fair to conclude, then, that Oral Roberts is disobeying God. And, finally, that Oral is deliberately using people's concerns over their health to build himself an empire.

In conclusion, it really doesn't matter what your salary is if you're provided a home, a car, an airplane, expenses, clothing, gasoline for your car, and sit at the helm of an organization that manipulates millions of dollars. It would even appear that Oral's reported salary has been deliberately placed below $30,000 just to make it sound low! When you add up all the luxuries that Oral has access to and take into consideration all the power he wields within Tulsa and Oklahoma, his "salary" and his power exceed that of men who make $500,000 per year.

Oral's influence and power

The power which Oral Roberts wields within Tulsa is rather well demonstrated by the following incident, relating to a dropped lawsuit. Southern Hills Country Club, for years, relied on watering its greens from wells fed by water lines which ran onto the golf course from the west side of Lewis Avenue. Riverside Investments, in the process of improving the banks of Little Joe Creek, west of Lewis, broke the pipeline that Southern Hills had used. There was a lawsuit filed on behalf of Southern Hills for damages because of Riverside Investments' apparent negligence in handling the creek-bank improvements. Riverside Investments, as you will recall, was one of the companies controlled by Oral's son-in-law, Marshall Nash.

On the morning that the suit was filed, the phone in the office of the attorney who had filed it began ringing off the wall. Finally the official for Southern Hills who had asked the attorney to file for the country club called him and requested that he drop the suit. The Southern Hills official told the attorney that Oral Roberts had called him personally and told him, "I want that lawsuit dropped before the day is over!" And the lawsuit was accordingly dropped.

Under the circumstances, Oral's ultimatum, and the acquiescence to it, reveals one obvious thing: Oral Roberts has a lot of clout! And he certainly has an inordinate amount of clout for a man on a mere $29,500 salary! Inasmuch as Oral's love for golf (and smooth greens) is rather well-known, one can only assume that his concerns over his son-in-law's business interests must have been greater.

Another incident relating to Oral's disregard for doing things according to the law relates to a culvert that the Oral Roberts Companies wished to have installed just south of property that currently is the site for the City of Faith project. The watershed on the City of Faith site, also adjacent to the University Village retirement center, was such that water backed up and made the 80-acre site a quagmire after heavy rains. The city of Tulsa did not have either the funds or the approval to put in a culvert which would cure the watershed problems, so Oral Roberts apparently decided to do it himself.

One ORU official informed Mayor LaFortune that Oral was going to solve his watershed problem himself. According to the official who told me the story, the Mayor shrugged his shoulders in tacit approval and asked, "What can I do?" Within the week, south Lewis, just south of 81st, was blocked off, a detour was run onto Oral Roberts property, and a culvert was installed under the street. Eventually, the street was repaved, the detour was removed, and traffic finally resumed as normal. All this was done on public property by Oral Roberts' employees at "company" expense, in spite of warnings from city officials that two of Oral's vice-presidents would be arrested if the street was torn up without obtaining the necessary permits. Excavation and re-routing was begun, and the two vice-presidents who had been informed that they would be arrested spent the weekend out of town!

Making money off the company

In addition to instances where Oral's relatives have made money by building some of Oral's projects for him, some of Oral's employees *also* make money by running business ventures which involve Oral Roberts University or the Oral Roberts Association.

One Oral Roberts vice-president whose wife has a jewelry business approached the ORU bookstore manager and asked to have his wife's line of jewelry put into the bookstore. The bookstore manager didn't think it was appropriate and told the VP that he didn't think it could be done. He then got a call from an ORU *Executive* vice-president who was a close friend and neighbor of the VP whose wife had the jewelry business. According to the bookstore manager, the executive VP asked him if he was having trouble making a decision about which line of jewelry to put into the bookstore. The manager replied that he wasn't having any trouble at all making a decision...he didn't think it was appropriate for an employee to have an "inside track" on bookstore business and that he had turned down the VP's request. Before the conversation was over, the bookstore manager was saying, "Yes, sir. No, sir" and agreed that the VP's wife should have her line of jewelry put into the bookstore. The jewelry sales in the university bookstore and the lobby of Mabee Center reportedly gross over $50,000 per year and provide a net income to the VP's wife of over $10,000 per year.

Another Oral Roberts Association vice-president who has an interest in a travel agency uses lists of prospective seminar participants, sends them mailings, indicating that their travel arrangements to and from Tulsa would be more conveniently handled through Tulsa. The man generates a lot of business in this manner. That person also arranged to have all of Oral's companies do business with his travel agency. Further, he made the statement that any employee who went on company business and used any travel agency other than his simply wouldn't be reimbursed by the company for their travel expenses!

The above executive also has an interest in a building on 51st Street in Tulsa, formerly owned primarily by Marshall Nash and, in addition to housing his travel agency, it also houses Marshall Nash, Inc., two detective agencies, and a private key club...*Suite 100.* How an official of a Christian university rationalizes having business interests that include relationships with private bars may puzzle some readers, but it probably comes under the heading of "Something Good Happening" to the vice-president who has such a business.

The show in the Prayer Tower

One fund-raising project being considered by Oral Roberts officials at the time of this writing has to do with a proposed letter to partners about the new multi-media "show" in the Prayer Tower. The presentation, entitled "Journey Into Faith," was a project I was placed in charge of about six months before I left Oral Roberts. It was little more than just one more example of Oral's predeliction for having his face, his life, his ministry, and his goals placed in front of the receptive eyes of tourists who visit the campus.

The multi-media, multi-room presentation is not at all unlike going through one of the theme shows at Disney World...such as the Hall of Presidents or the Haunted Mansion. The show starts out with Oral's background as a child, his early years as a pastor, the early tent meetings, the television ministry, the City of Faith project, and finally a rather nebulous impression of what the future holds for Oral Roberts and anyone who might be willing to practice the concept of Seed-Faith.

The cost of the project, as I sit here typing with budget projections in front of me, was well over $1 million. It seems patently ludicrous that such a sum would be spent on a project *that has absolutely nothing to do with helping people.* The money spent on that project won't be available for charitable purposes, it won't be available for student scholarships, it won't be available for the medical school, and it won't be used for medical research. The money spent on the project represents only one thing: a monument to the monumental ego of Oral Roberts. There is nothing in the show about people being helped, people being saved or people being healed...in a primary sense. Rather, the purpose of the show is designed to encourage hero worship directed toward Oral. At the time I organized the project, I made a statement to a fellow staff member that I thought the expenditure was an unjustified waste of financial resources and had nothing intrinsically of value to a *ministry.* I've seen the show and I still feel that way.

At an average of $5.00 a throw, it took 200,000 of Oral Roberts' partners to build that silly thing and when you learn of such ridiculous expenditures, it is little wonder that the Oral Roberts Association refuses to provide a financial statement to such organizations as the Better Business Bureau or the Chamber of Commerce. Doesn't it seem just a little odd that while most churches provide their congregations an annual financial statement, that the Oral Roberts Companies do not?

When you study all the revenue sources of the Oral Roberts Companies...direct mail, seminars, deferred gifts, wills and bequests from retirees at University Village, and income on investments...and I have the benefit of inside information obtained while having worked there...it boggles your mind to realize that the annual "take" of Oral's combined ventures since 1969 has been, on the average, approximately $60 million per year. Over a ten-year period, that becomes $500 million.

If the campus construction did cost $50 million as reported and you throw in another $12 million per year in salaries for the combined companies, the ten-year expenditure in the same time-frame as above would approximate $170 million. If one generously throws in another $10 million per year to be spent on television, the combined expenditures for that ten-year period approach $300 million. Whatever became of the remaining $200 million? Perhaps Oral has been putting a little aside all these years so he can build the City of Faith debt-free.

Ugly people aren't desired...
sometimes not allowed

It would seem appropriate, and certainly cause no one to lift an eyebrow, if a man like Oral, who had spent a lifetime praying for the halt and the maim, had a campus that had more than a smattering of people, employees and students with physical infirmities. Oral Roberts University, however, in spite of claims to the contrary, has always been rather coy in its relationships with handicapped people. Other than in Mabee Center, which houses the seminars where handicapped people are allowed to come to Oral Roberts for prayers, no building on campus was ever designed to accommodate the handicapped: no ramps for wheelchairs, no large stalls in rest rooms with handrails, and no parking for handicapped personnel. It wasn't until after being cited by HEW, that the University made some of the above changes to its buildings.

I once asked an Association official why there weren't more handicapped people around. In all sincerity, the fact that there weren't rather surprised me. I was told *that Oral Roberts didn't want them around*...and the person who told me that is a high-ranking official who is recognized within the companies as Oral's closest associate! I inferred two things from the man's statement about Oral's feelings toward handicapped employees: that Oral might not want them around because they might bother him by asking him to pray for them and heal them of their infirmities *or* that Oral didn't want them around because someone might begin to wonder why Oral *didn't* pray for all those people and get them *healed.* I'm not certain which of those inferences is correct, but I'm convinced one of them is.

It is a well-known fact within the Personnel Offices and the Student Affairs Offices that neither handicapped employees nor students are to be encouraged to come to Oral Roberts University. For several years, the Admissions Office wrote letters to prospective handicapped students, informing them that they would not be admitted because of being handicapped. If, as Oral Roberts says, God is at the center of the Oral Roberts University campus and always present at the point of people's needs, then it would seem that if a handicapped person could succeed *anywhere,* that it would be on the campus of Oral Roberts University. And further, if Oral Roberts really believed what he said, he would want to encourage handicapped people to come to his campus and begin letting miracles wash over them...making their lives richer, more rewarding and centered around God.

Overweight students have also been openly discouraged from applying for admission to Oral Roberts University. This has most recently been admitted by Oral Roberts on two television programs. One can only wonder what Oral's reason is for openly discriminating against overweight people. It is one thing to recognize, as most of us do, that being overweight is a health hazard but it is quite another to rather blatantly discriminate against someone whose weight is probably genetically predetermined and not due to an individual's wishes to be obese. One factor which might have a bearing on Oral's attitudes towards obesity perhaps stems from his attitudes toward his own mother. Pictures of Oral's mother reveal her to have been possessed of a rather obvious weight problem. And the treatment Oral gave his mother after she had retired in University Village made many people question just how kindly Oral felt toward her. Many of the elderly people living at Oral Roberts University Village can attest to the fact that on holidays such as Easter and Christmas, they would leave the village with friends or relatives to celebrate the day outside the institution...and there, sitting by the front door all by herself, would be Oral's mother, apparently overlooked for the day. Most of us know in our own minds how it would hurt our parents if, on important holidays, we did not either call, telegram, send flowers or gifts, or personally visit them. Inasmuch as Oral's home is less than five blocks away from University Village, it seems grossly inconsiderate that his mother would be left sitting alone in a lobby on a holiday.

In summary, the fact that Oral Roberts designs his television and direct mail appeals to people who need healing...while openly discriminating against them...tends to leave his true attitudes toward the sick open to genuine inquiry. Perhaps the real hypocrisy of Oral's attitudes *and his ministry* are revealed by such discrimination. He is willing to exploit the vulnerabilities of disabled people by sending them fund-raising mail, he designs his television programs to appeal to people who need a healing, and he is even willing to pray for them under controlled circumstances such as seminars where fund-raising is also involved. But, he is apparently unwilling to have them around, as either employees or students, in what might reasonably be expected to be larger numbers than average.

Chapter 12

The Heir to the Throne: Richard Roberts

As far back as 1968 when I first visited the campus of Oral Roberts University on a consulting trip relating to computer utilization, concerns were being voiced over what would happen to Oral Roberts' ministry if anything ever happened to Oral personally. While I perceived that the people who asked that question were more concerned over their jobs than Oral's ministry (if anything were to happen to him), the fact remains that the question is still valid today.

Oral Roberts, personally, is the most cunning, shrewd, subtle and devious man I have ever met. Based upon my observations and experiences while working with him, I would put him into the same league as Richard Nixon. Only *smoother.*

Richard Roberts, however, as heir apparent to the Roberts empire, is a horse of another color. While one might look upon "old Oral" as an experienced war-horse who's been through several battles, young Richard is more like a young, green-broke colt, poorly trained, bad-tempered, tender-mouthed, and altogether spoiled. Most of the people I've heard on campus who talked about the matter of "taking over the reins" have voiced the opinion that Richard just doesn't have what it takes to step into the traces and pull old Oral's burgeoning wagon.

Young Richard might be fairly likened to the stereotyped son of a hard-driving, domineering father...where the son never really gets a fair chance to stretch his wings, test his capabilities or develop his own real personality. Richard once told me personally that he really didn't understand how or why everything worked the way it did within his father's organizations. I understood what he was saying at the time, because there were moments when I puzzled over some of the same kinds of questions. In all likelihood, however, there would seem to be little doubt that anyone who doesn't have the name Roberts could effectively carry on the ministry that Oral has built up over the years.

As explained to me by one of Oral's top associates, Oral is very methodically setting an environment wherein Richard will be encouraged to eventually step in and assume increasing responsibilities. Creating such an environment has been, and continues to be, a gradual process wherein Richard gets a taste, a bite at a time, of more and more control and power. There are aspects of Richard's nature, however, which make many of Oral's people wonder if he'll really be able to handle it.

Work habits

One of the first steps taken toward getting Richard involved in the administration of Oral's organizations was to make him president of the Oral Roberts Evangelistic Association. When I left the organization, that title for Richard was still a titular position: his expense checks had to be signed by someone else, his ideas about programming had to be approved by other individuals close to Oral, and he still functioned as little more than a figurehead.

For one thing, Richard hasn't yet learned how to work. He never, in the three and one-half years I worked for Oral, put in a full eight-hour day for a full five-day week. There was always something...golf or tennis...which would take him away from the office or keep him from even coming in. And while he would sometimes test his authority by stating that he should have been consulted about this or that matter, it was always difficult to involve Richard in the administrative process. A true administrator has to be around to make administrative decisions. Therefore, most of the executive decisions necessary for a smooth operation within the Oral Roberts Association were made by other individuals who knew they were really reporting to Oral. Such individuals were always around during the normal work week and could be counted on to make decisions and then go through the perfunctory process of informing Richard, after the fact, that this or that had been done in his absence.

A typical example might be, "Richard, while you were out the other day, I talked with Jerry Sholes and he says that Tennessee Ernie Ford's manager is ready to sign a contract for our next TV special." Richard would reply, "Oh, Oh, Oh, that's good. You go ahead and set it up." He would often start to walk away and then, apparently thinking he should ask *some* questions, would query, "Ernie's willing to work for our standard pay, isn't he?" Assured of that, Richard would then head back out for Southern Hills and, from reports I heard, would tell golfing partners that he had just arranged for Tennessee Ernie Ford to be the guest on the next special!

Unwilling to work but needing to build some sort of positive reinforcement into his own mind, Richard often conducted himself in the above manner. On numerous occasions, after I had made suggestions to Oral's television producer about upcoming specials, the producer would talk with Richard, and *then* Richard would come to *me* and relate how the upcoming special would go! The entire arena of activities which involved Richard being allowed to take credit for things other people had done was a very special game that a select few of us had to play with him.

The creative game

If you ask Richard Roberts who selects the music for Oral's television specials, he'll tell you that he does. When I worked for Oral Roberts, if you asked Richard's music coordinator who selected the music for television shows, that individual would answer, "I do!" At least, that's the answer he would give you in private. If you were to ask him that question around Richard, he'd tell you that Richard picked the music!

In actuality, several people would suggest music that eventually was used on Oral's television specials. For "Oral Roberts in Alaska," the opening song was "In This Wide World," suggested by our director. In that same Alaska show, the John Denver song, "Come Fill Me Again," was used in the show on my suggestion...along with "I Can See Clearly Now." The song Richard selected for the show was "Grandma's Featherbed"!

The song used for the primary mood-piece in "Oral Roberts at Grandfather Mountain," was also one I chose..."Morning Has Broken." That mood-piece, accompanied by an early morning sunrise and beautiful nature footage was perhaps the most powerful piece of aesthetic video ever used on one of Oral's television specials. To this day, although we had some technical problems which affected video quality, I am still rather proud of the content of that show. The music which Roy Clark sang in that show was also done at my encouragement.

The point I'm leading up to, of course, is that neither Oral nor Richard are capable of providing much creative input into the formation of a television special. However, if people like the show, Oral and Richard are always "at the ready" to take credit for the development of their shows.

The creative game we had to play with Richard Roberts, for instance, was something we all viewed with quiet hilarity. Inasmuch as Richard knew that his father wanted him to provide creative input into the selection of music for the television specials, Richard had to be involved *somehow*. And here is the way it worked:

The producer would ask me to develop a show concept along with music suggestions that were compatible with a show theme or a sermon Oral wanted to use. I would put together a show treatment, complete with optional themes that included considerations for Oral's book offers. In addition, I would write treatment suggestions for music along with settings or location scenes that would make Richard and Patti look as good, for example, as their guest star. We always had to worry about that. We didn't want to get ourselves boxed into the intramural embarrassment of having made our guest star look too much better than Richard. That was a "no-no."

After I had written such a treatment, along with various options and suggestions for music, the producer and I would get together for a discussion. In such discussions, I often had to explain logic, aesthetics, and reasons for doing something this or that way to the producer. After I was sure the producer understood the show, I would be excused and he would then call Richard into his office. The producer and Richard would then go over a "suggested show."

Once the producer was certain that Richard understood the show and that he had made handwritten notes, Richard would go talk over the show and suggested music with Oral. In many cases, music tracks or records which I had obtained were routed through the producer to Richard...who would then, in turn, play them for Oral. Oral would either approve or disapprove of some item and changes would be made. Sometimes, Oral would suggest something that made no sense at all and the producer would call me back and ask my opinions on how to "clear up" conceptual problems that would, for various reasons, make the show less effective...because of something Oral wanted to do!

After those problems were ironed out, Richard and the producer would fly to Nashville to talk with their arranger, Ronn Huff. Most of those discussions were taped and I would be given copies, in the event that the arranger provided input that made sense. In those discussions, the pecking order was what made the whole procedure so comical. In *those* discussions with the musical arranger, Richard played the role of creative genius and would imply that the show ideas were *his*..."What I'd like to do, Ronn, is open the show with nature footage to the tune, 'Morning Is Broken' and be able to create a mood that is representative of the area and at the same time essentially religious in nature." *My words*. The three of them would spend hours discussing various things that often had nothing at all to do with the show and when Richard and the producer would arrive back in Tulsa, I'd be given a complete typed-out copy of their conversation.

The entire procedure was established by the producer to allow Richard to make it look as if *he* was providing creative input into the shows. Richard, when it comes to music, tends to shoot from the hip, become excited over one song, and not really concern himself with the overall effect of a show. Occasionally, when he really wanted to sing a certain song, it *would* get inserted into a show whether it belonged there or not. In any case, the games we had to play with Richard were enlightening and sometimes a little hectic. "Grandma's Featherbed" was one example. In the show, "Oral Roberts in San Francisco," we suggested, of course, that Richard sing the song, "I Left My Heart in San Francisco" and it was initially intended by me that it be used at the top of the show...to open it. During the pre-production stages of that show, Richard got it into his head that a musical "bridge" was necessary between his "San Francisco" opening and Oral's opening comments which were generally formatted into location shows...after the initial music. Neither Richard, the producer, nor Ronn

Huff, the musical arranger, had visited the location scenes where Richard was to sing his opening number...which was then to be followed by a natural segue through a dissolve to Oral and Evelyn standing at the top of a hill near the Golden Gate Bridge. In short, neither Richard nor his arranger knew what they were talking about. They didn't know that the combined effect of their musical "bridge" along with a video transition would not work if used between "I Left My Heart in San Francisco" and Oral's opening comments. Uninformed, they insisted, however, that the "bridge" be incorporated into the show, even though I argued against it.

When Richard saw the show after we had edited it together, he became furious. He called me personally on the phone and started chewing. I listened for a while and then began explaining it all over again to him...like I had to him and his producer before we ever attempted shooting the show. It finally came out in the course of that conversation that what he was *really* irate about was that he had told several of his friends in Tulsa that the San Francisco special would begin with him on the Golden Gate Bridge singing "I Left My Heart in San Francisco." And then, when he saw the show, and it *didn't* begin with him doing that, he was angry and told me, "It will look to my friends like I don't know what I'm talking about!" And while that was, indeed, the case, it was difficult to tell that to a coming 30-year-old whose father signed my paycheck!

Temper, temper

Oral's temper is rather well-known within his organizations and it should come as no surprise that his son, Richard, has one too. During one rehearsal for a taping, Richard became so upset with our director that he turned to me and asked, "Is he a director or a pussy?" I groaned a little because some of our ORU students on the set *could* have heard the comment and I then replied, "I really don't know, Richard. I think he's probably just trying to do his job."

I later learned that Richard was upset because he wanted to get his rehearsals over with so he could get out for a golf date! Golf is his game. He is a 3-handicap player on one of the world's most difficult courses.

On other occasions, when the production schedule called for Richard to come in at a certain time for camera rehearsals, he simply wouldn't be there on time. I'd begin phoning Richard's secretary, or his home, trying to find out where he was, usually without success. Several times he showed up over an hour late...and by that time, in order to conserve valuable rehearsal hours...we would sometimes be involved in blocking other numbers with the World Action Singers, etc. Good old Richard would walk in late, ask why we weren't set up to rehearse *his* numbers, and then he'd do one of two things. He'd either leave the set and not rehearse at all that day, or he'd demand that I change our already changed schedule so he could begin rehearsals. Regardless of which option he chose, he took no pains to let it be known that he was angry! Spoiled sons of men of God are sometimes hard to work with!

Richard, the director

At one point in Richard's development, he considered himself to be a proficient television director and, as will be revealed, his views of a director's responsibilities were somewhat limited. Up through 1976, all of ORU's basketball games were videotaped with Richard playing the role of director. He also "acted" as director for some of the coaches' shows that are still seen in Tulsa and are now produced by Channel 8.

At any rate, a director's responsibilities include pre-production meetings with the lighting director, the technical director, the cast, the cameramen, and the audio crew. While most of us sit in our easy chairs at home and take no thought about the tremendous amount of planning that goes into the

178

taping of any television show, you can rest easy in the knowledge that Richard Roberts views things the same way you do. The only difference being that he considered himself a director!

Richard, in acting out his part as a television director, had everyone else do the planning and the production work. He'd then walk in about 15 minutes before a taping was to occur and would expect everything to work like a finely tuned clock. If he didn't understand something...or didn't arrive in the control room soon enough to be properly briefed...he'd blame it on the personnel who had done the planning.

One time just prior to the taping of a coach's show, Richard started to chew out the lighting director on some minor issue and the lighting director (who was just about to leave ORU for a lighting job in Hollywood) cut Richard off at the pass by saying, "No, Richard, you're wrong! At best, what you're trying to tell me is simply a matter of choice. If you want to provide creative input into the formatting of this show, then you either need to come down here for our production meetings or make yourself available on the phone so we can get your input. But, don't expect to walk in here five minutes before taping and ask for all kinds of format changes that you could have suggested yesterday!"

Richard didn't say a word. I'm sure he was stunned that anyone had the nerve to speak back to him. At any rate, the lighting director left within a month or so after that and Richard wasn't able to get even with him. In fact, shortly after that, Richard decided he didn't have time to direct television shows anymore!

On another occasion, when Richard was directing the taping of several ORU student musical groups, he became angry with a couple of the cameramen...who were ORU students...and began verbally abusing them over the production line. This occurred during what is called the camera blocking stage, when the director is rehearsing with both the cast *and* the cameramen. Both the cast and the cameramen need rehearsals...so the cameramen can set up their shots. During such blocking, a knowledgeable director is very specific when he instructs a cameraman what shot to set up on. If he wants the cameraman to zoom in he should say, "zoom in," or "zoom out" if he wants a zoom-out at that point. Richard would just say, "Zoom, camera two," and if the cameraman zoomed in when Richard wanted him to zoom out, Richard would tell the cameraman off! And with his microphone on, so that every other cameraman could hear his comments, Richard would turn to his technical director and complain, "What kind of cameramen do you have me working with today? He should *know* that I wanted him to zoom out rather than zoom in. I mean *that's* stupid!" On that particular day, for those tapings, no one answered Richard and he finally regained his composure and continued blocking. What *was* stupid was Richard's actions and his own insecurities, *not* the actions of the cameraman.

I felt something would have to be done to keep Richard from making further mistakes like that and after the taping I took him aside, rather carefully forming my words. "Look, Richard," I said, "You're Richard Roberts and some of these cameramen are students. They look up to you, and what you say and the way you act has a tremendous effect upon the way a taping goes. When one of your cameramen makes what you consider to be a mistake, you need to know that criticism from you can really hurt that person's feelings. You forget that you're not 'one of the boys.' You're Richard Roberts. When someone makes a mistake, have them correct the shot, and when they have it the way you want it, compliment them. You'll get a lot more out of them and everyone on the set will be able to work under less tension."

Richard left the studio later that day and told a close associate that he liked working around Jerry Sholes, that working around me helped him. What I'd done, in very simple terms, was to convince Richard that when cameramen made mistakes (because of improper instructions from *him*) that it wasn't his fault. With that insecurity taken off his shoulders, Richard was able to relax for the next two days of taping and almost acted like a competent director.

Richard's vindictive side

In the summer of 1976, Oral's producer called me on the phone and said, "You're going to have to fire 'so-and-so.'" For purposes of telling about this incident, we'll just call the young man John Doe. John Doe, at that time, was our stage manager. I asked the producer why I had to fire him. The producer responded that he really didn't know why, except that the young man had done something to upset Richard. I then told the producer that the young man, John Doe, had a number of talents and that I really wanted to keep him in the organization and I then asked if I could put the man into another slot. The producer replied, "Yes, but whatever you do, keep him out of Richard's sight. And find another stage manager right away."

Not having any idea what the circumstances could have been that led to Richard's anger toward John Doe, I called the young man into my office and just laid it all out for him. I informed him that Richard was angry with him for some reason and that he could no longer be our stage manager. I then informed John Doe that I had been in the process of creating another job, anyway, in another area within the television production department and asked the young man if he'd be willing to step in and take over that job. The young man was understandably hurt by the incident, but shrugged and indicated that he really didn't have any choice...and that he would take the other job.

I then asked the young man, "Why is Richard upset with you? Did you have a problem with him on the set during rehearsals?"

He replied, "No, we got along fine. I don't think my stage managing had anything to do with it."

I then replied, "Well, John, *something* happened. Richard had to have *some* reason for wanting me to fire you."

Young John Doe then told me that he knew why Richard wanted him fired. Patti, Richard's wife, had called him up to the house for a massage. Her back had been bothering her and she had learned that John Doe had worked as a part-time masseur at a health spa while attending another college before transferring into ORU. John Doe had been giving Patti Roberts a backrub on her living room couch when Richard walked into the house.

I asked John, "You're telling me that Patti called you up to their house...that you were giving her a backrub on a living room couch, and Richard walked in. That nothing improper was going on, but that Richard didn't like it. Is that right?"

John replied, "Yes, that's right. Richard didn't say anything, but I could sense that he was annoyed. He just walked right on through the living room and didn't say a word."

I then asked the young man, "John, how old are you?" He replied that he was twenty-one. I put that together in my head along with the knowledge that Patti was two years older than Richard, had two children, a fine home, and every reason not to do *anything* improper, let alone form some alliance with a male ORU student who was at least six to seven years her junior.

My opinion of Richard, at that point, went down about ninety-three points and I concluded my conversation with the young man by giving him the following advice: "You have this other job as of now and I'll process the paperwork today. However, you're to stay out of Richard's sight *totally*. In the meantime, you're to communicate only with me and other personnel within this department. And if the skies ever clear on this matter, I'll let you know when you can come out from under wraps."

The young man agreed to the terms and it was nearly six months before Richard found out that John Doe was still working for me. By that time, the young man had developed a reputation in his new job of being thorough, of planning productions carefully, and of using good judgment. At that point, there was no way the young man could be fired. I should say that at the time all this happened, I did not personally like John Doe...but I did respect the way he went about getting his work done. And while I don't wish to take any credit for the fact that the young man did his job very well...and is still on the payroll in television production...I will indulge myself in one small bit of human expression that may be a weakness on my part, *"Ha, Ha, Richard!"*

Although it is difficult to define a man's lack of administrative ability, hopefully these first-hand experiences (among many) will demonstrate why those who must work with Richard are most aware of his shortcomings.

Succession—a real problem

Millions of people are attracted to Oral Roberts, personally and financially. People are not personally attracted to Richard and he has no track record as a fund raiser. He even has the further disadvantage of being known as a singer, an entertainer, a performer...not the proper background to step into the shoes of a healer chosen to do God's work. When the Board of Directors sits down to decide who should take Oral's place as the head of the company, there will be few votes for Richard. But there will also be a total lack of names on the list of those who can step in and do Oral's unusual work.

This lack of succession is very serious for if funds are not raised from the multitudes around the world, the entire structure collapses. It will be many years before the expensive City of Faith project can even approach a break-even position. Without Oral, attendance at the University is bound to diminish. The many loyal Oral Roberts lieutenants around the world will not automatically transfer their allegiance to Richard as they would lack the faith in the young man's ability to get results.

At this writing, however, there seems to be no one else being groomed for the job. The future of the Oral Roberts Ministry, under Richard, does not look too bright. This fact should be of vital concern to the City of Tulsa which could well end up with one of the largest concrete elephants in the world at the southern extreme of the city limits. Oral Roberts at age 61 is not in the best of health. Insurance statistics give him less than a decade to get his empire in condition *and* train an able replacement. This must certainly be the number one priority before the Board of Directors and it will be interesting to see which course is selected. The sands of time are running out and Richard is showing no signs of being able to attract support as the new king, even though there is no clear competitor seeking the nomination. The City of Faith is such a tremendous gamble at this point that it might well be the case that no successor in his right mind would want to accept the job if offered. Oral just might have begun a project so vast, risky, unacceptable and, in many respects, downright foolish that others do not want to fill his shoes now.

There is a very basic, ministerial problem here. It is part of the healer's Bible to preach the fact that God selected him to do His work. The healer did not make the basic decision — he was chosen to do it.

This important fact lends creditability to the entire ministry and precludes the healer from passing his "gift" along to his son. At the very least, Oral would have to have a conversation with the Lord about the need for nepotism and then announce to the world that God had decided to choose Richard as his successor. On a recent program, this orderly transition from father to son seemed to be underway. Richard took credit for having healed a woman's toe. Honestly...it was her toe. This seems to carry on the old tradition that one must start at the bottom and work his way to the top.

The unfortunate part of the entire matter of transition from father to son is that Richard does not personally portray the role of a healer or even a religious minister. He has a pleasing, baby face totally lacking Oral's ability to roll the eyes and mesmerize the viewer. He did not inherit as much of his father's charisma as he did his mother's charm. Richard is now divorced and lacks an all important partner. This is definitely a partner-type business inasmuch as the leader does have to come home at night and at least occasionally have dinner with his spouse and perhaps talk over the events of the day. Richard, as head of the Oral Roberts Evangelistic Association, would require a very understanding wife. It may be very difficult to find another Evelyn.

Chapter 13

Oral Roberts
Running Scared

On Wednesday, March 7, 1979 (there's that number seven *again*), an ORU employee whom I had worked with called me and indicated that Ron Smith, Chief of Staff for Oral Roberts, wanted very much to meet with me as soon as possible.

I asked, "What about?"

He replied, "Ron said something about you writing a book about Oral Roberts and he wants to talk with you about writing another kind of book. I want you to know I'm just a middle man on this but Ron explained a deal to me that sounded pretty good. *Real* good, in fact, and I think you ought to listen to what he has to say."

I then asked the ORU employee, "Ron Smith is having you call me just because he wants me to write a positive book about Oral Roberts?"

The man replied, "Well, there's more to it than that. Some of it involves some business deals that sound pretty sweet to me. Ron did say that he and Oral had talked about it...you writing a book for them...and Oral agreed that Ron should contact you."

I replied that I wasn't very high on Oral Roberts...that I thought his bucket had lots of holes in it...but that I would meet with Ron Smith and listen to what he had to say. The above employee arranged a meeting between us at the Village Inn on south Yale at 10:30 a.m., Thursday, March 8, 1979.

In the course of my conversation with Ron Smith, he stated that he wanted to make it quite clear to me that what he was offering was not a bribe of any sort to keep me from writing *this* book, that he and Oral had discussed the need for a *new* kind of book about Seed-Faith...one written by a former employee of Oral Roberts. In that conversation, Ron indicated he could give me all types of examples, letters from partners, business deals that had been successful, etc., as a result of Seed-Faith.

What Ron Smith offered me was a $10,000 advance on a $25,000 stipend to write the above book. In addition he offered me a position as writer for a stock-buying newsletter, wherein he would give away information about thinly traded stocks that were priced below book value. In his stocks/bonds newsletter, he would enter into buying agreements with newsletter subscribers and encourage them, on a given day, to *all* buy the same stock on a given day at a given price. Such activity across the country would tend to force a stock *up*. His portfolio plan for potential subscribers to the newsletter would be for all of them to let the purchased stocks ride up 2.5 points and then they'd all sell and make money.

I asked Ron Smith if he'd already be sitting on shares of stock when he advised subscribers to buy. He replied, "You betcha!" For writing the newsletter to his subscribers, Ron Smith was going to pay me 25% of the profits and he indicated that he was, at that time, netting $30,000 per month on the stock market. That much money would have netted me $7,500 per month merely for writing a stock-dabblers newsletter! When I got back to my home, I asked my calculator just how much money that was per year. My calculator responded that it tallied out to $90,000 per year...just for writing a newsletter! I've written a lot of things in my life, but I've never made *that* much for doing so *little*.

The conversation then shifted back to the book that I was encouraged to write about Oral Roberts. Ron indicated that if I was writing this book for *money*, that I could make a lot more by writing his book, rather than the one you're presently reading. He then stated, "You're a writing genius, but I'm a marketing genius. We have the capability to market over a million books. Your book probably won't sell any better than Wayne Robinson's *Oral* did. It *might*. But, I can tell you that it takes a pretty big organization to market over a million books."

I indicated that I wasn't writing this book for money and that I wasn't very much inclined at all to write a positive book about Oral Roberts...regardless of how much money I would get paid as the author. I did state, however, that I would like to sleep on the offer and I would call him back the next day.

I didn't really have to think it over and when you read the last chapter in this book, you'll probably understand why. I called Ron Smith back the next morning and made the following statement. "Ron, I've decided that in all good conscience, I cannot write the kind of book you described to me. I would, however, be willing to become involved in the personal deal you mentioned...writing the stock newsletter for you. That sounded pretty good."

Ron replied, "Well, no, I couldn't do that. If you can't do one, you can't have the other. At least, not right out of the gate; I just don't see how I could do that at all. It looks as if we'll just be travelling in different directions...and I'm going to just keep on practicing Seed-Faith."

I then asked, "Ron, let me ask you *one* thing. In our conversation yesterday about Seed-Faith, all you discussed was making money. Why does *everything* about Seed-Faith always revolve around money. And why does it *always* involve suggestions that people give Oral Roberts money?"

He replied, "Well, people relate to the dollar. They want to get ahead and when you show people how they can be successful and be Christians, they listen."

188

"Ron," I queried, "what does a dollar *really* have to do with being a Christian?" He replied that such a discussion wouldn't get either one of us to change our minds and I agreed, wished him good luck, and hung up.

Within two weeks, Gary Gibson, the Chief of Security for Oral Roberts University called on my publisher and warned him that I was involved in "secret" negotiations with Oral Roberts...that I was planning to write *another* book and in it, I would denounce everything in *this* book.

My publisher, a little aghast at receiving such a visit from Oral's Security Chief, thought Mr. Gibson's remarks were a little odd for two reasons: 1) he knows how serious I am about this book and 2) he didn't think that Oral Roberts would allow his Security Chief to be openly discussing the matter if I *were* negotiating such a deal on another book. Oral's Security Chief then told my publisher that he shouldn't give my book too much credibility because I was just a disgruntled former employee of Oral's.

My publisher was familiar with *that* line also. Oral Roberts, for example, called his former Dean of Medicine an "angry man" because that individual left for professional reasons rather clearly articulated to various people within the Tulsa medical community.

Anyone who leaves Oral Roberts for what they consider to be good and sufficient reasons is labelled either "angry" or "disgruntled."

Regardless of whether I am or am not angry or disgruntled isn't something that's really known by anyone but me...and any denials I might make will necessarily be viewed with some question. I accept that.

However, my own opinions and actions have never been as interesting to me as the actions and opinions of other people. And I find it *extremely* interesting and, I might add, just a little flattering to learn that a man whose primary responsibility is Oral's *security* would harass my publisher *after* I had turned down an offer to write a positive book about Oral Roberts.

I *know* that what I'm writing in this book is true. So does my publisher, so does Oral's Chief of Security, so does Ron Smith, and so does Oral.

Chapter 14

The City of Faith

As difficult as it is to accept...and I had some problems with this myself...the City of Faith *is based upon lies*. The shocking fact is that Oral Roberts, *personally*, is responsible for those lies. Further, the nature of the lies...having to do with Oral making statements about how and when God told him to build the City of Faith and even what to name the complex...leaves Oral Roberts open to a rather well-deserved public contempt. Because of personal involvement on my part in the promotion of the City of Faith, and because of my participation in various planning and strategy sessions relating to the City of Faith, I *know and am witness to the fact* that Oral Roberts has personally lied about the City of Faith. Those lies and the nature of them...Oral telling millions of people that God told him to do something...are what made me decide to write this book. Everything in this book, every chapter, would have gone to the grave with me, unrevealed to anyone, if it weren't for that fact.

During my professional life, I have worked for several educational institutions, and I have always been a loyal employee. I accept the fact that, in open competition with other institutions or businesses, we all play "the game" to a certain

191

extent and, in most cases, the end justifies the means. However, there is a "line" beyond which most professionals working for an institution or business will not step. For *me*, that line is something you step across when you deliberately tell a lie, in God's name, and exploit a vulnerable public from the sinecure of religion.

Within the next few pages...and this chapter is really what this book is all about...it will be demonstrated, *beyond any doubt*, that Oral Roberts has personally misused his public trust, abused the sanctity of his purported relationship with God, and deliberately misled millions of his partners and the public *with at least two outright lies.*

The announcement lie

On September 7, 1977, Oral Roberts announced the City of Faith...making it quite clear in his announcement that God had told him to build it and to put 777 beds in the hospital. *There's that number seven again.* In making his announcement, Oral conveyed that he had experienced *a vision in the desert in August 1977,* and that *God had spoken to him and had given him all the details for the three building complex* which comprised the City of Faith. Also, Oral said that God had told him...*in the desert in August 1977*...that the three buildings in the complex were to be: a hospital, a clinic and a research center.

However, in JANUARY 1977, Oral Roberts and Ron Smith, Oral's Executive Vice-President, met IN MY OFFICE and discussed WITH ME a three building complex which would include a clinic, a research center and a hotel...which would eventually be converted into a hospital. That discussion took place BEFORE Oral's announcement and 7 months BEFORE he had his "vision" in the desert.

In that conversation, Oral Roberts personally stated that he thought it would cost over $100 million to build the complex...and that as he improved his personal fund-raising skills, he *"needed to find thicker fleece to pick."* That's a verbatim quote from a "man of God."

We discussed some of the unique construction aspects of a hospital...such as oxygen lines being available in all rooms...and we concluded that such construction could be incorporated into the "hotel" and be available for use when the "hotel" was converted into a hospital. Hospital affiliation for the training of students and residents was, even then, viewed as a temporary arrangement to be tolerated until the medical school was smoothly functioning. We even went so far in that conversation as to discuss unit costs on the parking lots which would surround the three building complex.

During that conversation, we also discussed potential management problems in running a hospital and Ron Smith agreed to contact executives of Hospital Corporation of America. Oral told Ron Smith to approach that discussion with the understanding that Oral Roberts' companies would retain ownership of the hospital and that HCA could have management responsibilities only.

Oral then indicated that he planned to meet with the owner of a large hotel chain and discuss having that chain draw up plans...and perhaps oversee construction...of a facility that would be compatible with conversion to a hospital.

Nothing about that conversation bothered me, at all. It was strategy designed to head off any possible problems with hospital affiliation that could, in turn, affect the accreditation or curriculum of the medical school. Most people would agree that the above conversation is part of "the game" I mentioned earlier.

The thing that turned me off...and made Oral a calculated liar...is that in his October issue of "Abundant Life," he clearly stated that *everything* about the City of Faith was revealed to him in a vision he had in the desert. The desert where Oral said that God spoke to him was his million dollar home in Palm Springs and he was there in August 1977.

However, the conversation Oral Roberts had with Ron Smith and me in my office about a clinic, a research center and a hotel which was to be converted into a hospital occurred in January 1977...*seven months before Oral had his "vision"*; eight months before he publicly announced the City of Faith and nine months before he lied to his partners in the October issue of "Abundant Life" and told them that God had laid everything about the City of Faith before him!

The lie about the name for the three building complex

In the conversation which occurred in my office, no mention was made of a name for the three building complex. In the October '77 issue of "Abundant Life," however, Oral Roberts made this statement about his August '77 vision: "Suddenly God gave me a new name for the Health Care and Research Center I am to build in His name. You shall call it the City of Faith."

CORONET magazine in 1955 published an article entitled "God Heals—I don't" which also quoted Oral Roberts as having purchased 175 acres in Tulsa for the purpose of erecting "The City of Faith." At this time it was being referred to as his new Corporate Headquarters. That article, incidentally, was written by Phil Dessauer who is the current managing editor of THE TULSA WORLD. Both the article and the newspaper's editorial policy were very supportive of Oral Roberts' activities.

In May, 1956, an article, "King of the Faith Healers," appeared in AMERICAN magazine which revealed that Oral Roberts had just purchased a 175-acre site for $250,000 and there he intended to erect a whole City of Faith."

If God didn't reveal the name "City of Faith" to Oral until August '77 why was he using it in 1956?

It is indeed revealing, and more than a little disappointing, to learn that Oral Roberts is capable of stretching the truth in any manner. It is absolutely unforgivable, however, for Oral Roberts, viewed by millions as a true man of God, to *deliberately lie* about God having spoken to him. In my humble estimation, there is *nothing* lower than using the authority of God as part and parcel of an outright lie.

It will do Oral Roberts absolutely no good to deny what I have written here. In the one instance, I have documents to prove that the term "City of Faith" goes back as far as 23 years and can be traced to Oral Roberts. In the other instance, relating to the conversation Oral had with me in my office, any argument would boil down to my word against Ron Smith's and Oral's. Before God, however, as I sit here typing this, what I am writing is the truth, along with everything else in this book.

The law and the hospitals

The following paragraphs about the laws which govern hospital construction and expansion may seem rather dry, but I implore you to wade through them so that further sections in this chapter will put the City of Faith into perspective for you as a taxpayer and a consumer of health services.

In 1974 the National Health Planning and Resources Development Act was passed. Usually called Public Law 93-641, it states that the need for a hospital, hospital expansion or addition of a service must be *demonstrated*. The law was designed to prevent unnecessary duplication of hospital facilities and services which increase health care costs. The law requires that state health planning agencies study demonstrated needs and determine what should or should not be built. If justified, a Certificate of Need is granted.

In Oklahoma, there are two "agencies" which operate under the authority of federal laws to govern the operations of hospital facilities: 1) The three member Oklahoma Health Planning Commission (OHPC) was established by Public Law 92-603 and has primary responsibilities for reviewing Section

1122 of the Social Security Act. Under Section 1122 of the Social Security Act, hospitals may recover from Medicare/Medicaid patients that portion of their bill attributable to capital expenditures, such as debt reduction and depreciation of facilities. Inasmuch as many hospitals in Oklahoma, like any other state, provide a broad range of health services to people who qualify for Medicaid/Medicare payments, the board which oversees those payments has a lot of clout.

That board, in Oklahoma, is the OHPC, chaired by Lloyd Rader. As chairman of the three member OHPC, he has the power to audit hospitals, review charge sheets and approve or disapprove Medicare/Medicaid payments. For many small hospitals in the state, and for some not so small, a disapproval or a temporary "hold-up" of a Medicare/Medicaid payment can mean the difference between a hospital being in the black or in the red for a given month. In other words, as chairman of the OHPC, Lloyd Rader has the power to hold up Medicare/Medicaid payments and financially "pinch" a hospital and, through audit procedures, he can create a threatening environment to a hospital's administration.

2) The other agency in the state is comprised of a 30 member Board of Trustees and, as both consumers and providers of health services, they collectively make up the Oklahoma Health Systems Agency, the OHSA. While the OHSA and the OHPC have both been created as a result of federal laws, state law requires that the OHSA (the 30 member board) review applications and submit recommendations relating to Certificates of Need to the OHPC (the three member board) and *that* board makes a final decision.

The following events have occurred up to this date with regard to the issuance of a Certificate of Need for the City of Faith: the OHSA (30 member board) has a review committee comprised of full-time staff members. This review committee has primary responsibilities for reviewing and analyzing applications for Certificates of Need. In addition to an extensive staff analysis, the review committee conducted a public hearing on February 9, 1978, heard a full day's testimony from both sides of the issue and accepted mountains of documents as evidence. After careful deliberation, the review committee recommended to the 30 member OHSA board that the application for a Certificate of Need for the City of Faith be disapproved on Feb. 16, 1978.

The 30 member OHSA board then conducted two hearings on the proposed hospital for the City of Faith and heard both sides argue their respective points about a new 777 bed hospital in Tulsa. ORU officials entered an amended application whereby they asked for only 294 beds and proposed to "shell in" the remaining hospital facilities. Under that motion, a separate Certificate of Need would be required if the full 777 beds were desired by City of Faith officials.

The 30 member OHSA board voted against the substitute motion and by a vote of 19 to 6, recommended to the three member OHPC board that the application be denied. On March 2, 1978, the three member OHPC returned the City of Faith application to the 30 member OHSA for further study after ruling that the reduction in dollar amounts and bed totals did not constitute sufficient change to warrant refiling the application.

At about that same time, ORU's City of Faith officials submitted new information relating to its application and on March 16, 1978, the 30 member board met, considered the information, and voted once again, recommending to the three member OHPC board that the Certificate of Need not be granted.

The *initial* hearing set by the *three member OHPC board* for March 22, 1978, was *rescheduled* and when that board met on April 26, 1978, a Certificate of Need was granted to Oral Roberts for his City of Faith. On the surface, it seems rather odd that the three member OHPC (chaired by Lloyd Rader) would grant a Certificate of Need after the 30 member OHSA board had conducted such extensive hearings and made two recommendations that the Certificate of Need not be granted. However, the information revealed below will, perhaps, make the actions of Mr. Rader's three member OHPC board more understandable.

Strategy sessions with ORU officials

The week following February 9, 1978, when the review committee recommended that the 30 member OHSA board turn down a Certificate of Need for the City of Faith, I met with two high-ranking ORU officials at their request. Those officials were Ron Smith, Chief of Staff for Oral Roberts and Dr. James Winslow, Vice-provost for Medical Affairs for Oral Roberts University and the City of Faith.

In that meeting, my opinions and suggestions as a public relations professional were solicited. Having worked as a behind-the-scenes lobbyist for one of the three Regent institutions in Iowa, I made the following general suggestions to Ron Smith and Dr. James Winslow: 1) that the Oklahoma press be courted and treated favorably by ORU officials, 2) that all 30 members of the OHSA be identified and their professional backgrounds obtained...where they lived, where they worked, who they worked for and who, in their respective communities, had the kind of clout that they would respect *and* determine if any of the people who had clout in the above communities felt favorably toward ORU and the City of Faith, 3) identify legislators who felt favorably regarding the City of Faith application and ask them to contact as many of the 30 members of the OHSA board as possible, 4) determine who on the 30 member board were providers and/or consumers of health services and then attempt to establish relationships (relating to potential City of Faith services) that would make the above members respond favorably, from a community standpoint, to the City of Faith application, 5) elicit public support from as many prominent legislators as possible, including those at the federal level, and finally, 6) inundate both agencies and Oklahoma legislators with mail supporting the City of Faith from partners in Oklahoma.

The reason for the meeting was made clear before my suggestions were sought. Dr. James Winslow told Ron Smith and me that Rader had told him he'd have no problems with the application at the three member board level. However, Rader had told Winslow that he didn't want to be "out there on a limb" all by himself and that something had to be done to get more support from the 30 member board: get a favorable recommendation, if possible. Ron Smith complained that one of the problems with the 30 member board was that too many of them were providers of health services and that the City of Faith application for a Certificate of Need was considered to be a threat to the financial viability of health service institutions around the state. He then indicated that if it was up to the state legislature, an application would probably be approved. I suggested that perhaps he could get someone to pass a resolution favoring the City of Faith.

Later, such a resolution was passed by the Oklahoma legislature. The resolution, however, was not written by *any* Oklahoma legislator. It was written in Oklahoma City *by Ron Smith* and, according to a later account, it was written *in then-Lt. Gov. Nigh's office.* Several witnesses heard Ron Smith make that statement and, as you might remember from the press, Lt. Gov. Nigh was present at the ground-breaking ceremonies for the City of Faith.

The conversation then centered for a time around Winslow's frustrations in taking accurate notes during the conversations he was having with Lloyd Rader. It was very apparent that Lloyd Rader and Dr. Winslow had a relationship based on common goals: getting the application for the City of Faith approved. Winslow made the statement that if he had a recorder on his phone, he wouldn't have to worry so much about taking good notes as he was talking with Rader. Ron Smith then picked up the phone and told another vice-president of Oral Roberts Association to have a phone with a recorder installed immediately in Dr. Winslow's office.

James Winslow then asked Ron Smith if Oral realized what might be necessary to get more support going for the City of Faith application. Ron Smith replied, "Oh, well, he probably knows but he can't be involved in those kinds of things. We'll probably just have to go ahead and do some things that we won't tell Oral about." Dr. Winslow then mentioned his concerns over the application and its effect upon the Liaison Committee for Medical Education (the LCME) which was going to be reviewing ORU's medical school facilities, curriculum, and faculty staffing. Inasmuch as the LCME is a quasi-official group governed by HEW, Winslow also expressed concern over what HEW Secretary Califano's position would be if the tempest ever reached that level. Ron Smith replied, "Don't worry about Califano. He used to represent Oral in Washington and he is on our side." (Califano's law firm represented Oral's interests in certain areas and, as far as I know, still does.) I was impressed with the evidence that a lot of quiet groundwork had already been laid much in advance of the eventual construction of the City of Faith.

Letters to the editor

Ron Smith then turned to me and stated that in addition to courting the press, he felt the need for something to be done, through a letter to the editor, which succinctly expressed what he felt to be the selfish interests of those who were opposing the City of Faith application. He asked me if I would prepare a letter to the editor wherein I likened Oral to Gulliver and made everyone opposing him seem like the Lilliputians...the small people. He further indicated that the letter to the editor had to be done by a real writer and that it should have a satiric vein and make readers snicker at the opposition to the City of Faith application.

That evening I wrote an open letter to the editor and forwarded it to Ron Smith. He then distributed it from his office, over my name, to several papers and TV stations in the area. It appeared, among other places, in the *Oklahoma City Journal* and *The Tulsa World,* and was read by Clayton Vaughn on Channel 6 in Tulsa. While it is a minor issue, my letter to the editor wasn't really that in the traditional sense of the word. I didn't send it to any newspaper myself. Rather, I wrote it as a staff member and it was then distributed to the press by an official of Oral Roberts University.

The following Monday, Ron Smith called another meeting and present were Bill Roberts, Vice-president for Construction; Ruth Rooks, Oral Roberts' personal secretary; Jack Wallace, Dean of Students; Carl Hamilton, Vice-president for Academic Affairs; James Winslow, Vice-provost for Medical Affairs; Ron Smith, Chief of Staff and me.

In that meeting, lists of the 30 member board were distributed and everyone began offering suggestions about people they knew in the hometowns of the members...people who might be able to put some pressure on the board members. We were particularly interested in identifying bankers, trustees of institutions where the "providers" on the OHSA board worked, county politicos and anyone else who was perceived to have clout in the respective communities of the OHSA board members.

Of the people present in that meeting, Jack Wallace and Bill Roberts knew more people around the state than any others present and they made several suggestions and agreed to make contact with various people on their own. Carl Hamilton indicated that arrangements had been made to have several bus loads of ORU personnel make the trip to Oklahoma City for the OHSA hearings conducted prior to and on March 16, 1978.

Also discussed in that meeting was the direct mail piece being prepared to go out to all of Oral's partners in Oklahoma. Again, the problem was mentioned that, because of another huge Association mailing, the City of Faith mailing might not be feasible in time to do any good.

It was decided that there was no possible way the mailing could be sent out and give partners time to write in to their legislators and have it do any good. The question was then asked, "When does the three member board meet?" When told that the three member OHPC board (chaired by Lloyd Rader) would be meeting on March 22, Ron Smith asked, "I wonder if that meeting could be set back?"

The March 22 meeting of the three member OHPC board was later rescheduled to April 26, 1978. By the time that board met, a mailing had been sent out by the Oral Roberts Association, and legislators and Lloyd Rader were inundated by mail from Oral's partners all over Oklahoma. The mailing which the Association sent out mentioned specific things about the City of Faith application and asked the partners to write to their legislators and OHPC members. A list of OHSA and OHPC members was included within the mailing.

Pictures of Lloyd Rader appeared in *The Tulsa World* showing him reading all the mail he had received in favor of the City of Faith application!

On April 26, 1978, the three member OHPC board, chaired by Lloyd Rader, met and approved a Certificate of Need for the City of Faith...in spite of mountains of data which clearly indicated that a new 777 bed hospital was not needed. The fact that Tulsa hospitals already had a combined 1000 bed excess...beds not being economically utilized...was disregarded and the application was approved on religious grounds. In view of the lies that Oral Roberts told about how God had spoken to him regarding the City of Faith, it seems quite reasonable to conclude that religious grounds were unjustified.

Serious contradictions

The negative impact of the City of Faith, regardless of whether it opens with 294 beds or 777, is probably understood by only a handful of people within the state of Oklahoma.

Oral Roberts and his representatives have repeatedly stated that their patients will come primarily from outside the state...that the City of Faith will be primarily a tertiary care hospital...meaning "final"; that people will come to Tulsa's City of Faith either to die or to be admitted there when all other health care institutions have been unable to provide the patient with a cure. The application for the Certificate of Need, however, revealed the hospital to be an acute care facility...and acute care facilities all over the country primarily serve patients from their immediate area.

In the process of carefully analyzing the application for the City of Faith hospital, the OHSA sent inquiries to every other HSA board in the country. Because those responses from other HSA boards around the country *were not* politically motivated by *either* side of the City of Faith controversy in Oklahoma, I personally attach a great deal of substance and integrity to them. Some of them follow:

Texas: There is some contradiction in the "tertiary care" objective when compared to the services that will be offered by the City of Faith.

Pertaining to the City of Faith stance that its facilities will not affect health care in the state...that its patients will come primarily from outside Oklahoma...Kansas made this comment: "Any bed addition not absolutely necessary will impact the health care system of the entire nation."

The Arkansas HSA board made a similar comment: "Additional beds could unfavorably impact underutilized hospitals. Any significant reduction in patient load of already existing facilities might result in reduced utilization."

The Louisiana HSA board had this to say: "It seems unreasonable to define the City of Faith as a 'tertiary care center of major national importance.' The City of Faith has not appropriately calculated need/demand for the services to be offered."

Rather overwhelmingly, the Health Systems Agencies from other states around the country agreed with the findings of the

Oklahoma Health Systems Agency. Why then, after the OHSA spent countless hours in review, analysis, and investigation, did the three member board chaired by Lloyd Rader act in opposition to the OHSA's findings and decide to approve the Certificate of Need for the City of Faith?

The situation is not entirely clear. Ron Smith, then Oral's Chief of Staff, told me that Rader not only supported the City of Faith project, but that he had it in for St. Francis Hospital in Tulsa and W. K. Warren, who was responsible for the financing and construction of St. Francis. Warren is known in Tulsa as a philanthropist — he donated property to the Catholic Church for the Vianney School for Girls and also encouraged Waite Phillips to donate the land where the Southern Hills Country Club is now situated. In addition, he'd contributed millions of dollars previously to Tulsa's St. John's Hospital, the largest in the area before St. Francis was built.

According to Smith, Lloyd Rader became angry at Warren and St. Francis *after* the passage of Public Law 93-641...the law that made it necessary for hospitals to demonstrate need before they could expand hospital facilities. However, a "grandfather clause" in the law allowed hospitals that already had signed construction bids in hand to proceed with current expansion without obtaining approval from state agencies such as OHPC or OHSA. St. Francis Hospital had already signed a contract with a Texas firm in 1972, before the law went into effect, so proceeded with its planned expansion without consulting Rader's office. This allegedly angered Rader, because he felt his office should have been consulted.

Officials at St. Francis confirm that their institutions experienced a surprisingly extended, costly audit at the hands of OHPC financial investigators subsequently, but are reluctant to speculate as to the motives behind the audit. They do note that no attempt was made to interrupt Medicare/Medicaid payments during the audit period, although the hospital's accounting in this area was being questioned. The audit failed to turn up any evidence of irregularities in St.

Francis' billing for services to be reimbursed through Medicare or Medicaid.

It is clear that Lloyd Rader was favorable to the idea of the City of Faith, that he exercised on its behalf. But that he exercised influence in a fashion that went beyond the properties of official conduct on the part of a public administrator is not clear. Questions do remain, however, as to the reasons for his evident initial conviction that the City of Faith project was one that should proceed, notwithstanding objections from other hospitals and health-service agencies in the Tulsa area. *The Oklahoma Observer* indicated its feeling that Rader's attitude was probably the outgrowth of personal concern shown him by Oral Roberts at the time Mr. Rader's wife died. Whatever the situation, in the months since first publication of this book, Lloyd Rader has been noticeably less supportive of the City of Faith...perhaps because of a deeper realization of all issues involved.

Nonetheless, at the time I discussed this with both Ron Smith and Dr. Winslow, it was obvious they were functioning with the comfortable conviction that Mr. Rader was on their side.

The City of Faith and the courts

Within a few months after the OHPC issued the City of Faith its Certificate of Need, the Tulsa Hospital Council filed a suit against the City of Faith and the OHPC on grounds that the legal criteria by which the OHPC was to rule on Certificate of Need applications had not been followed. And, further, that by issuing a Certificate of Need on religious grounds that the First Amendment had been ignored, and that the doctrine of separation between church and state had been overlooked.

The criteria which Public Law 93-641 established for reviewing applications for Certificates of Need follow:

1. Demonstrated need that an affected population has for a proposed health care service.

2. The availability of less costly or more effective alternative methods of providing such a service.

3. The immediate and long-term financial feasibility of the proposal as well as the probable impact of the proposal on the costs of (and charges for) providing health services by the proposing institution.

4. The relationship of the proposed services to be provided to the existing health care system of the area.

5. The availability of resources (including health manpower, management personnel, and funds for capital and operating needs) for the provision of the services proposed to be provided and the availability of alternative uses of such resources for the providers of other health services within the area.

The judge who heard the suit, in comparing legal criteria against the ORU application, rendered a decision against the City of Faith: that the criteria had not been followed and that the issuance of a Certificate of Need on religious grounds was a controversion of the First Amendment. City of Faith officials appealed to the Oklahoma Supreme Court and the case will be heard in the fall of 1979.

Christ in the Temple

There are certain aspects of the controversy surrounding the City of Faith which are basically ridiculous. Most of us ascribe great powers to God and in our own understated ways feel that if God was *really* on someone's side, that person would run into no opposition from anyone. The fact that Oral Roberts has had so many problems with his City of Faith concept would, all by itself, lead many of us to suspect that perhaps God really wasn't on his side.

Knowing, however, as I do that Oral Roberts has told and written calculated lies about non-occurring conversations with God, I am convinced that God cannot be on his side.

It would not surprise me at all to learn that Oral had suddenly found himself embroiled in circumstances similar to those which befell the money-changers in the Temple. And it would surprise me even less if I were to be informed that someone, in Christ-like fashion with a big whip in hand, had driven him permanently out of the Temple.

Perhaps the Oklahoma Supreme Court has what it takes to accomplish just that.

Epilogue

A Final Word

There are several federal and state agencies which act daily in the best interests of American consumers. Cigarettes, as a potential health hazard, cannot be advertised on TV anymore. Toys for children have to be safe before they can be marketed. Advertising which appeals to children has to meet strict guidelines. And, when we go to borrowing money for that new car, home or boat, the lender is required by law to inform us what the true annual simple interest rate actually is.

In other words, it is very clear that millions of Americans need protection from certain kinds of businesses and certain kinds of advertising which appear on television. Television is a *powerful* medium and, as such, the programming aired can serve either the common good or it can be detrimental to the best interests of a vulnerable public.

In my opinion, people are extremely vulnerable when their religious beliefs in God are involved. And when such persons' religious beliefs get intermixed with concerns over their health, their family, their financial state or any other problems which might cause them to turn to God, it is all too easy to exploit their predicaments.

Such exploitation is despicable. And one doesn't have to point to such extremes as the Jonestown madness to prove that some kind of governing legislation is warranted in order to protect the sanctity of our respective religious beliefs.

God should not be mocked by television, direct mail campaigns or "religious" magazines that are really designed to do little more than bring in millions of dollars to be spent at the whims of religious "leaders." And if it takes government regulations to protect us from such organizations, then perhaps we should write our elected officials and ask them to do something about it.

Perhaps such legislation could begin with these words from the Bible: "Beware of the scribes, which desire to walk in long robes, and love greetings in the market, and the highest seats in the synagogue, and the chief rooms at feasts; Which devour widows' houses, and for a show make long prayers: the same shall receive greater damnation."